Understanding the Secrets to Career Advancement

Understanding the Secrets to Career Advancement

Through the Eyes of an HR Director

David DiMartile

iUniverse, Inc.
Bloomington

Understanding the Secrets to Career Advancement Through the Eyes of an HR Director

iUniverse books may be ordered through booksellers or by contacting:

iUniverse
1663 Liberty Drive
Bloomington, IN 47403
www.iuniverse.com
1-800-Authors (1-800-288-4677)

Because of the dynamic nature of the Internet, any web addresses or links contained in this book may have changed since publication and may no longer be valid. The views expressed in this work are solely those of the author and do not necessarily reflect the views of the publisher, and the publisher hereby disclaims any responsibility for them.

Any people depicted in stock imagery provided by Thinkstock are models, and such images are being used for illustrative purposes only.

Certain stock imagery © Thinkstock.

ISBN: 978-1-4697-9510-2 (sc)
ISBN: 978-1-4697-9511-9 (hc)
ISBN: 978-1-4697-9512-6 (e)

Library of Congress Control Number: 2012904628

Printed in the United States of America

iUniverse rev. date:3/27/2012

Contents

Introduction

When I think back on my thirty-seven years of work, the last five of which were leading the Canadian HRM activity for a major, global automotive manufacturer, I believe I had a very successful career. The parts of my career that are most memorable to me are those times when I was able to play an important role in leading change in the business and helping people achieve goals that were thought to be unachievable. Accomplishment brings such a wonderful feeling that it becomes contagious. Being in a leadership role and being part of something bigger than oneself also brings great satisfaction if it is managed right.

The question is this: How do you get there? How do you make your way into the positions that will allow you to lead change, manage a business, head up a project, and get into a position where you can bring your skills and talent to help a company succeed and at the same time bring personal satisfaction to yourself?

Not everyone will make it into the position of his or her dreams. Not everyone has the skills to lead. But everyone can develop the skills to be successful—if he or she wants to and is prepared to do what it takes!

You can start by understanding what companies already understand about career advancement. If you hope to end up in a leadership position or in a position of interest, you need to understand what companies are looking for. There have been a lot of books written about how to take control of your career and set personal goals, but unless you know what companies are looking for, none of it will matter. You need to understand the things that will make a difference today and tomorrow that will allow you to control those variables that will impact your career.

1

That's what I will give you on the pages of this book.

And with that, I dedicate this book to *your* future success, and I am thrilled to know that I may have played a small part in your personal achievements.

Good luck!

David DiMartile

Chapter One

Do You Have a Job or a Career?

In any successful business, managers and employees share one common trait: they see themselves as having a "career" instead of a "job." What's the difference? In a career, the leaders, managers, and employees all understand what it takes to satisfy their customers. Each individual within the organization knows what his or her particular role is for achieving that goal of customer satisfaction. Employees at all levels understand and accept that employment stability comes from the success of the business, and if the business fails, so do they. People who have a "career" rather than a "job" understand what it takes to meet the goals of the business as a whole.

People who see themselves in a *job* believe that they have a defined set of tasks or duties, and when their work is done, they can sit back and relax or go home. People with "jobs" believe that when the end of their workday comes, it is time to go home regardless of whether their tasks have been completed for the day or how it affects the customer or the business. People with "jobs" believe it is the manager's role to give them more work if they are idle; they won't seek out opportunities for filling their unused time with activities that will improve the business as a whole. People with "jobs" believe they are entitled to their paycheck and their job simply because they complete their daily tasks or duties, regardless of what happens to the business.

People who see themselves in a *career* understand that they were hired to bring a skill set to help the success of the business. People in "careers" understand that being effective requires an understanding of the business—

its goals and the needs of its customers. People with a "career" need to understand the challenges that the business is facing and what they can do personally to overcome those challenges. People who see themselves as having a career understand and accept that their individual success is directly tied to the success of the business as a whole, and they take personal responsibility for helping the business become as successful as possible. I worked with several individuals who excelled in being role models for what a career stands for. These people were in key roles with responsibility for separate aspects of the business. These individuals knew and demonstrated to their staffs that it was not okay for their part of the business to be successful if it meant that other parts would not be. They understood that the whole organization had to be successful in order for their part of the business to be considered successful. To them this meant that it was important to understand the decisions that were being made in their part of the business, including how those decisions would affect others and, most importantly, how they would affect the total business performance and the customer. It was also important that everyone knew where help was needed and that everyone used his or her resources to assist in those areas. Basically, these leaders taught others to treat the business as if they were owners.

Now, it's important to note that not all business leaders themselves understand the difference between careers and jobs. In order for employees to behave as someone in a "career" as I just described, the business needs to have a certain kind of work environment. The success of this work environment is totally dependent upon the culture of the business. Some business leaders only allow their employees to have "jobs," in which case, that business will have the culture of workers who pack up at the end of their scheduled shift and employees who only do the bare minimum of what is expected of them. The leadership of the business owns the culture, and the leadership gets the culture it deserves.

The "Job" Business Culture

How do you know if you're working in a business culture that is only allowing employees to have "jobs" rather than careers? Here are some typical signs

I have observed over my career that demonstrate this style of business culture:

Many business leaders believe that employees are responsible for how they behave, involve themselves, share ideas, and look for opportunities to improve the business, "regardless of the way leadership behaves." In essence, they try to pass on the responsibility for the culture of the organization to the employees. I knew one leader who tried to make employees' attitudes and behaviours a part of their performance review and would not discuss with his employees why they felt and acted the way they did.

Many leaders and managers blame employees for what they see as a negative culture, and they even ask employees what employees can do to improve the culture of the organization (clearly an indication that those leaders don't believe they have any responsibility or impact on the culture). In one area where I worked, it was obvious that employees were frustrated with their leadership, as no one communicated with them, no one shared information with them, and no one asked them for their ideas or input on any part of the business. Employees believed that the leaders were going to make all the decisions, including how work would be performed, and the role of employees was simply to follow the leader. Obviously employees felt disempowered, but what frustrated employees the most was when leaders would blame employees when things didn't go right!

Many leaders are very good at providing employees with negative feedback or calling out mistakes in public, thinking that if they embarrass the employees, then they won't "screw up" the next time. These leaders don't provide positive feedback because they think they don't have to—after all, employees are paid to do a good job, right?

Other leaders simply do not understand the basics of positive reinforcement. They may tell employees that they "did a good job," but they don't elaborate and explain what the employees specifically did that was done well or what behaviours they would like to see again tomorrow. Sometimes leaders give feedback related to the outcome of the assignment rather than what each employee did to achieve the result. Without clarity, the leader risks reinforcing the wrong behaviour. I once witnessed a leader call his group together to provide what he thought was positive reinforcement. The leader called out a number of individuals and began to thank them for their success on a recent project they had completed. What the leader didn't know was that one of the individuals who was called out had actually been opposed to the teams' efforts and had worked behind the scenes to prevent the changes from being implemented. As you can imagine, this had the reverse effect on the other employees because they knew what this individual had done—and here the leader was including him in this recognition event!

Many leaders spend their time managing the technical aspects of their business and assume that the people side will take care of itself. They believe the only important thing is accomplishing the task or building the product, but they fail to understand how an employee's attitude based on the organization's culture can impact how the task gets done. I worked with a leader who was excellent at measuring and monitoring the performance of the business. The leader worked hard to ensure that all the right technical information was collected and reviewed and that technical changes were implemented when they were supported by data. This same leader was convinced that if he managed the technical aspects of the workplace, then performance would take care of itself. In reality, the technical part of the production system was fine, but employees were dissatisfied with how they were treated by their supervision and, accordingly, did the bare minimum they needed to stay out of trouble. In fact, regardless of the technical changes and the additional investments made, leadership was unable to increase the output from this production system. The leader's reaction was that the employees had bad attitudes, because all aspects of the production system were in place and output had not increased; therefore, he felt discipline should be used as the means to change employees' attitudes. When discipline was in fact used, employees rebelled and output from this system went down. Clearly, the culture that existed in that case was not going to be fixed by further changes to the technical systems.

Many leaders have a different expectation for themselves and hold employees to a different standard, believing that, as leaders, they should have more "liberties" because of their role or position. These same leaders often see the resources of the business as theirs to do with as they please.

Some leaders (who are workaholics and get rewarded with bonuses and stock options) have an expectation that their employees (who do not get the same economic treatment) should work the same hours, be available at night and on weekends, forgo vacations, and be responsive and involved in ongoing business during their holidays. They believe that if they have to be available at all times, then they should have access to their employees as well. I worked with a group of leaders who actually bragged about the amount of time they spent working or doing e-mails or conference calls while they were on vacation. When their employees heard what the leaders did, they perceived that what was valued by the leader was working when you were not physically at work. In actuality this had two negative effects: first, employees would start bragging about the work they did when they were off (even if they didn't actually do any work), and second, those individuals who had strong values and tried to maintain an appropriate level of work-family balance either gave up on their careers or began looking at other companies that actually valued work-family balance. As you can probably guess, the individuals with the greatest talent and potential were the ones who were most successful in finding alternate employment when in fact these were the individuals the company could least afford to lose.

Some leaders are poor listeners (a very common trait) and cut off employees in the middle of their delivery or shoot down their ideas or suggestions without hearing all that the employees have to say. These leaders believe that because they are in a leadership position they must be smarter than their employees; after all, if they weren't smarter, would the organization have put them into that position in the first place?

Many managers believe that they only need to share information with employees that is relevant to their job (these people also believe that information is power and it helps them keep employees in line by giving themselves an advantage over their employees).

Some leaders give employees assignments without telling them what the parameters are or what the expected outcome is. When the assignment doesn't meet their expectation, they then blame the employees for their "incompetence," rather than blaming their own lack of specificity. I was coaching a leader several years ago, and we had several discussions on the effect of empowerment on changing the culture of an organization. One day this leader decided that instead of having his leadership team decide how they were going to structure the shift schedule for the production system, they would gather a group of employees and give them the task of deciding. Several individuals were selected from across the organization, and they were told that they should meet to discuss and decide what the shift schedule should be for the production system. Unfortunately, they were not provided any other parameters. The team came back to leadership and told them that they had done a survey and each department had selected the shift hours and arrangements that they wanted to work and that they wanted to implement the new schedules the following Monday. When confronted with the outcome from the assignment, the leader immediately said no because there had to be only one shift schedule for everyone, because the payroll system was not capable of handling several different schedules, and because the decision submitted would have a negative impact on the customer. Obviously the team was shocked by the reaction! Why? Because the leader had not shared the parameters with them in advance *and* the leader had told them that they were empowered to decide, not to bring back a recommendation. Unfortunately, this situation had a very negative effect on this leader's future ability to empower other teams going forward.

Some leaders believe that employees should have to go through the same work experiences that they went through in order to be effective in their role or to have valid ideas or input. These leaders believe that the knowledge only comes from specific experiences, and they fail to look at other ways employees learn. I worked with a leader who happened to have a limited formal education and was now in charge of a group of people who were responsible for making engineering changes in support of the production system. A new employee was added to this leader's group, and this individual was a recent Harvard grad. Shortly into their work experience together, the leader involved the Harvard grad in an assignment to reengineer a work station that was creating a bottleneck on the assembly line. Without the leader's knowledge, the Harvard grad went out and talked to the employees who worked at this station to get their input regarding what changes could be implemented to best achieve the desired outcome. The changes proposed were simple, inexpensive, and could be implemented almost immediately. When the Harvard grad returned to the offices to report on the status of his project, the leader told him that the idea was ridiculous and that he needed to find a technical solution to the problem. The leader told the Harvard grad that he hadn't been around long enough and didn't have enough experience to know that his simplified solution would not work but that the leader did and, based on his experience, another, more appropriate, solution was needed. (The Harvard grad went back to the group of employees on the work station, and they quickly made the changes they had discussed and demonstrated that the simple solution did in fact work.)

Some leaders believe that employees who do not contribute their ideas or take on more work are simply lazy and will not be effective if promoted. A leader in this category generally does not talk to his employees or try to understand employee perceptions of the work environment and what is within the leader's control. I knew a leader who was very negatively perceived by his employees, and all the data, such as employee surveys and transfer requests, showed that the leader did not value his employees. I learned that this leader did not have any regular communications with his employees, nor did he ever have any casual conversations with them individually about the workplace. Subsequently I was at a Human Resources Management (HRM) Committee meeting (where decisions about employee careers and promotions and such are discussed) and I was surprised to see this same leader become adamant about his perception of a number of his employees. What surprised me the most about this situation was that his perceptions were totally based on his view of how those employees shared their ideas and communicated with him! I knew several of the employees and had received feedback on them when they had worked for other leaders, and clearly his perceptions were different. This leader had created a culture in his part of the business that left employees out and on their own, and now he was using his perceptions to try to influence the careers of those individuals who were impacted by what he created.

Many leaders believe that employees have to excel in every assignment in order for them to be considered as "having potential" for advancement, even though the skill sets for the positions may be different. When I worked at one of our assembly operations, we had implemented a career-development process to help give some developmental experiences to individuals we believed had talent and were promotable. One typical experience we planned was to have engineers spend some time supervising in production. The purpose behind this was to give the engineers some firsthand experience in dealing with how production employees have to live with what engineers design and to give them a new set of insights that they could bring back into their engineering assignments. In this process some leaders developed a mind-set that an engineer who was not successful in managing the production assignment and dealing with production employees should no longer be considered as "having potential" for future promotions. It took a tremendous amount of education to convince these leaders that just because these individuals were not successful in production that did not mean they couldn't be successful in an engineering role, especially if they were a subject-matter expert and were not required to supervise others.

The "Career" Business Culture

How do you know if you're working in a business culture that values employees and offers the opportunity for a career rather than a job?

Some managers are effective at building relationships with their employees (both personal and professional). These managers understand the importance of having a good relationship and how it enhances the ability to solve problems and understand perspectives in dealing with complex issues or problem situations. I worked with a leader who believed he needed to spend at least one hour per day just talking with his employees.

He believed (and the performance in his department supported this) that getting to know his employees and developing a relationship with them helped him understand their thought process and their value system and their risk tolerance, etc., and that each of these factors made it easier for him to understand the feedback that he received from each of his employees and also helped him decide the types of assignments that each of them would excel at and enjoy.

Some managers understand that their role is to help employees by providing support, removing roadblocks, setting direction, reinforcing positive behaviours, and measuring performance. These leaders understand that to maximize the benefit for the organization the leader must utilize the efforts of all employees, and they understand that the role of the leader is to act as the maestro. In one of my assignments I got to know two highly talented leaders who were assigned to manage critical parts of the operation. One leader was focused on his success and spent most of his time overseeing his employees and ensuring that they did things correctly, and when they didn't, he would intervene and do the task for them. The second leader also spent most of his time observing his employees, and his interest was ensuring that each employee understood his or her role and the outcome, and he allowed the employees to decide how they were going to achieve the end result. He also made himself available to discuss approaches, to provide help, and to guide employees to others in the group that they could learn from for a specific activity they were undertaking. This leader also spent time measuring the performance of his employees and looking for opportunities to provide positive feedback and to call out the specific behaviour that the individuals demonstrated that he would like to see again tomorrow. After a short period of time, the overall assessment of these two leaders' methods was unanimous: the leader who empowered his employees not only accomplished more but also had more satisfied and dedicated employees. In addition, the performance of the group in total far exceeded the results of the other leader's group.

Some managers share important information about the direction, goals, and strategies of the company and involve employees in identifying objectives to help the company meet its goals. These leaders have a clear understanding that in order for employees to make effective decisions they need to know where the leadership is trying to take the business and that employees will follow the priorities if they are known to them. In one of my assignments I was exposed to a leader who excelled at sharing information with his employees and helping them understand how what they did fit into the overall performance of the business. The reputation that was developed for this leader was that his group was exceptional at reacting to problem situations and finding solutions that were in the best interest of the total business. His employees understood the concept that they were responsible for helping the business be as successful as it could be. (This leader also had the highest demand for his employees to be reassigned to other departments.)

Some managers look for opportunities to provide positive reinforcement to their employees and to celebrate "wins." Leaders who follow this philosophy understand that all employees want to be recognized for their accomplishments as well as their efforts, regardless of who they are or where they are in the organization. They also understand that when you reinforce a specific behaviour or action, you increase the likelihood of it being repeated again in the future. These leaders know that by clearly articulating the action or behaviour being reinforced they also help other employees understand what leaders value, and this, too, increases the likelihood of other employees demonstrating those same actions and behaviours in the future. One time a good friend of mine approached one of his employees in the open office area and told him that he was impressed that the employee had gone out of his way to learn what the competitors were doing to deal with a specific situation and used that as his base line to come up with a way to enthuse his customers. He also told the employee that his ideas and efforts allowed the company to increase its sales well beyond the forecast levels. Subsequently, a number of employees who had observed this employee receiving positive reinforcement also began to look externally at competitors for ways to improve internal methods. These individuals not only learned from the positive experience they observed but also wanted to receive positive reinforcement themselves and accordingly modified their behaviour in order to get it.

Some managers provide constant feedback to employees and provide support to help them develop. These leaders understand that the more they help develop their employees the more likely the employees are to have the desire and the knowledge and skills to assist when those competencies are needed. This has a positive impact not only for the employee but also for the organization.

Some managers have career discussions with employees and try to influence their employees' careers in line with their interests. These leaders understand that employees need to have input into where they want their careers to go (they have to live with the outcome, and it is their careers that we are talking about). These leaders also understand that employees will be more aligned with the business if they believe that leaders have their best interests in mind.

Some managers use mistakes or errors as opportunities for employees to learn, and they sit down and debrief the situation with employees and figure out what could be done differently to get a better result. These types of leaders understand that it is critical for employees to feel safe in taking calculated risks; employees need to know that if they try something and fail that they won't be discharged or reassigned. If employees do not feel safe, then mistakes will be hidden or covered up—or worse yet, no one will take calculated risks for fear of failure. (Note: This is not to say that there will never be a negative reaction to mistakes or failure. If actions are deliberate, if employees ignore the advice or direction of leaders, or if the same mistake is repeated, these instances may result in a negative reaction, and I believe employees can understand and accept that differentiation.) I experienced a situation where an employee was sent out to deal with a customer complaint. After listening to the customer's situation, the employee decided that it was appropriate to replace the product for the customer. The customer was enthused! Upon his return and learning what the employee had committed to, his leader called him in to discuss the way he had handled the customer complaint. The leader was supportive of the effort and direction of the employee's actions but was concerned about the potential cost impact to the company. The leader and the employee had an open discussion and learned from each other several important lessons. The first lesson was that it was right to try to satisfy the customer. Second, the employee should have had an exploratory discussion with the customer to understand his or her expectation. Third, alternatives that were less costly should have been explored first before a decision was made to replace the total product. After the discussion, the leader again thanked the employee for his effort and for satisfying the customer. This turned out to be a tremendous learning experience for this employee. Instead of being turned off for potentially doing the wrong thing, the employee took his newfound knowledge and used it to develop a deeper relationship with customers and at the same time improve the company's reputation and reduce costs.

Some managers believe that they are the role model for their employees and that they should be held to the same or even higher standards. These leaders understand that employees look at their leaders and try to figure out what they value, not by what *they say* but by what *they do*. They understand that their employees should see them as demonstrating the behaviours that they expect in others and that employees should be held accountable for demonstrating those behaviours. Many years ago I had the misfortune of witnessing a key leader choosing to use company resources for his own personal needs. The situation involved having employees spend time and materials to make something for his personal use that the leader was not able to buy on the open market. The leader had rationalized that because they were using scrap materials it was okay—no harm, no foul. The following week I learned of a situation where an employee in the same shop was caught working on his own time using company equipment to make something for his personal use. I was called by this same leader, demanding that this employee be discharged for using company equipment for his personal use! This became my opportunity to have this leader learn from his mistakes.

Some managers believe that they need to provide employees opportunities to learn and grow so that they may give them larger assignments and opportunities—especially when time becomes critical. Again, these leaders understand that the more they help develop their employees, the more likely the employees are to have the desire and the knowledge and skills to assist when those competencies are needed. In one of my previous roles we would initiate employee feedback surveys to help gather information about how employees felt about various aspects of the employment relationship, their work environment, and their perceptions of how leadership was handling a variety of situations. One key learning that we took away from these surveys was that many employees were interested in learning new things and having new experiences. Employees wanted to be able to contribute more and were willing to learn in order to be able to do so. This feedback became a terrific avenue for HR to explore with leaders the opportunities to have cross-functional assignments and to use cross-functional teams to deal with problems or concerns that were facing the business. Once started, we received so much positive feedback from our employees that we formalized the process whereby individuals could make their interest in participating known to leadership. In the HRM meetings many leaders commented about how positive this initiative was for our employees, but they also had witnessed many of their employees benefiting from these experiences with new knowledge and new skills that could be applied to other aspects of the business.

Some managers are exceptional at providing assignments and setting boundaries and outcome expectations when communicating with their employees. These leaders are experts at empowering their employees. They understand what employees need to be able to take on an issue, provide their full knowledge, experience, and creativity, and deliver outcomes that are within the boundaries set by leadership.

What You Can Do When You Work in a "Job" Culture

What happens if you are working in a company or business where the culture does not value employees or their participation? What if you are working in a business culture where the employees all have "jobs" rather than "careers"? You have to make a choice. You can either leave that business to try to find one that *does* value the contribution of employees and has the business culture you are looking for or you can stay and try to get into a position where you can change the culture of the current organization.

If you choose to stay, at a minimum you can be the lone voice in the crowd that talks about the virtues of a different culture—a business culture that values employee ideas and involves them in the business beyond their current set of tasks and duties. You and I both know that leaving a challenging work environment is the easy way out, and it does say something about your ability to deal with tough challenges. True leaders don't run from challenges; they embrace them and strive to overcome them. (This is not to say that employees should not pursue career interests with other companies, but they should view a career change as an opportunity to move forward, not a way to "get away from" what they are experiencing.) Several years ago a very talented and respected leader in the organization wanted to have a discussion with me. The leader had observed that regardless of the efforts that she placed on trying to create the right kind of culture for her employees, the company leadership was making decisions and exhibiting behaviours that did not take into consideration the effects on people. She thought that because she had made some progress in her part of the business that her employees would be satisfied with "their culture," and she was surprised to learn that many of them, although happy in their work groups, were still dissatisfied with many aspects of the company. Because of this she was struggling to decide if this was the right company for her to work for the rest of her career. Our discussions led us to having more formal discussions with her employees and using that information to provide feedback on how employees were feeling about the actions and behaviours of senior leaders. The result of this activity wasn't that employees became thrilled about every decision that leadership made, but leadership agreed to put a process in place to sense-check decisions with a pilot group of employees before any formal decisions were made. Not perfect, but some progress!

The kind of culture that exists in each company is truly a function of the people in the company. The culture is mainly formed by how employees react to what they believe leadership values, not by what they say but by what they do! Only you can make the right decision for you. We all contribute to the culture, and as such we can influence it over time. The higher one goes in a company, the greater one's influence will be. But changing the culture of any organization is no small task and happens over a long period of time. So if you choose to stay and you want to make a difference in the culture of the company, you need to know that what you are signing up for is a lifelong commitment. The rewards that come from having a positive culture are tremendous from a business as well as a personal perspective. The effects of having a negative culture can be devastating both to business results and to employee attitudes and levels of commitment.

If you see yourself as having a career versus a job, I can help you achieve your career goals. If you see yourself as just having a job, you will find the advice necessary for you to take the steps to make your job feel more like a career, whether you choose to stay in your current position or move to a new one.

Chapter 2

Defining Success in Your Career

During my career, one of the most frequent discussions that I had with other employees dealt with how to "get ahead." Getting ahead meant different things to different people. Some people felt that getting ahead meant landing a new position in another area of the business with new responsibilities; some people wanted what they considered to be more fulfilling work or to make a bigger contribution to the organization; and some people felt that moving up the corporate ladder or into a supervisory role was their definition of success.

Regardless of how each person defined "getting ahead," what everyone really wanted to know was how business leaders made their decisions. Why did one employee get selected or promoted over another? In talking with these people, I heard a lot of stories and tales about certain people in the organization being preselected for a promotion or a position. Management might post notices about vacancies within the organization and go through the motions of interviewing a variety of other candidates, but the individual selected for the position was known in advance.

People asked questions about why seniority, or length of service, in an organization wasn't used as the basis for selecting people, because the general belief was that people with the most years in the business would automatically have the most knowledge and experience.

I heard challenges from individuals who thought they should have been promoted because they were the "best" at what they did and that qualified them for advancement.

To understand success in individuals' careers, we have to look at people's skill sets and abilities to see which of the three categories of career paths they are best suited for:

1. ***Individual contributor:*** Works in a nonsupervisory position with a degree of responsibility (for example, engineer, accountant, staff assistant, sales representative, purchasing agent)
2. ***Manager of people:*** Supervises people in performing a specific activity on behalf of the organization (for example, production supervisor, engineering manager, advertising manager, payroll supervisor)
3. ***Executive:*** Directs a business function and works with other functional executives in executing business strategies (for example, director of sales, engineering director, chief financial officer, human resources director)

Not everyone fits into all three categories; in fact, most people don't. Research has shown, and my own experience has certainly validated this, that there are different competencies, skills, and abilities that determine the likelihood of success in each of the three categories.

There are some competencies, skills, and abilities that overlap, but the predominant competencies for each category are different. So what is a competency? For our purposes we will define a competency as having an ability to perform an activity at a high level using the required skills and appropriate behaviours. Some examples of competencies include "managing conflict," "customer focus," and "negotiation skills."

Not all competencies, skills, and abilities exist in everyone. In fact, there are some competencies that very few people in the general population possess. And yet these are the exact competencies, skills, and abilities that are most desired and in demand by companies.

Some competencies, skills, and abilities can be taught; some can be learned through experiences; and some you either have or you don't.

With a better understanding of these competencies, you can begin to see that each of us can be successful in one of the three categories. Having the competencies (skills and abilities) for success in one category but not the others does not mean you are a bad person or a failure; it simply means that you have tendencies, skills, and abilities that will lead to a more successful career in one category versus the other.

Many people have a false belief that to be successful you have to advance to the top leadership or management positions in business. Having an understanding of how most people have skills and abilities for success in just one of the categories shows us that moving someone who is most competent in the "individual contributor" category into a management or leadership role will likely lead to dissatisfaction, frustration, and failure for both the person and the business. In one of my operations assignments we had a manager in our maintenance area who had been considered one of our best tradespersons. This individual had the most technical knowledge and could perform virtually any maintenance task and had been well respected for his abilities. When he was promoted into the management ranks he struggled because he could no longer perform the work himself and now had to rely on others to accomplish those tasks. Additionally he was now required to spend a considerable part of his day organizing the work plan, responding to critical equipment breakdowns, and doing payroll and other tasks normally required of any supervisor. After a period of time, this manager came to realize that he was not spending his day performing tasks that he had the skills for and loved to do; instead his day was spent performing administrative activities that he found totally unsatisfying. By mutual agreement we reinstated the manager back into his tradesperson role, and his attitude toward work returned to its premanager level. This individual knew that he wanted to be successful in an individual contributor role, and returning to his former role made him successful.

It's no different than in other aspects of life. Some individuals have the skills and abilities to be successful as a quarterback or a tennis player or perhaps a pianist. But no one has the skill set or ability to be good at everything! The most important learning that we need to take away from this is that if people are placed in a role that requires certain competencies, skills, and abilities and they lack those skills and are unable to develop them or alternatively develop a strategy that allows them to function effectively without them, they will most certainly be unhappy, frustrated, and unable to add value or be as successful as they would if they were in a position best associated with their skill set.

[The following competency descriptions are my interpretation of the work of Michael Lombardo and Robert Eichinger, who performed what I believe to be the best research on the subject of competencies and their relationship to careers and success. From this point on I will reference their work through the term "competencies," otherwise known as Lominger competencies.]

Before we explore the competencies that differentiate success between the three categories, it is critical to understand that there are some competencies that span across all positions. In order to be considered for career progression in any one of the three categories you first have to demonstrate proficiency in the basic competencies.

The basic competencies are not considered differentiators for selecting people for advancement, but they do create the first impressions. If you can't get the basics right, no one will take a chance considering you for higher-level positions, even if you believe you have the greatest skill set in the competencies that matter in a defined category.

Do the following competencies describe your personality, characteristics, and workplace actions? If not, you will need to develop these basic skills and abilities before pursuing career advancement in order to increase your potential for success.

Trustworthy: You are widely respected and known for being open, honest, and truthful. People confide in you because they know you will keep the information secret and confidential. You are someone who doesn't varnish or twist the truth in an effort to protect your reputation and will openly admit mistakes when you make them. Despite being someone who is constantly looking to improve yourself, you only present information in an appropriate manner and will never act or behave in a self-serving manner at the expense of others. I knew a leader who was running a production area who was having difficulty getting the required amount of parts from the production system. At this time we had a restriction on working overtime. When his director learned that his area was not producing at an acceptable level, he challenged the leader to work with his team to find ways to resolve the problem and increase their output. In order to meet the demand for additional parts the leader unilaterally decided to have his team work overtime, and he was determined to find a different way to pay his team for their time worked instead of using the payroll system, which would make his actions visible. On the following Monday, his director approached him and thanked him for finding a solution to their output problem. At no point did the leader tell his director that the extra output was performed on overtime. Approximately two months later, the director learned of the leader's actions, and when challenged about the situation the leader simply responded that he had not been asked how the extra parts were achieved. This obviously was unacceptable, and the leader lost his credibility with leadership, putting an end to his career.

This competency is what I call a show stopper. If you are not seen by others to have integrity and you are not viewed as being trustworthy, you will struggle in all your work relationships and have great difficulty getting things done. It is extremely difficult to think that others would question our integrity or that they don't trust us. The good news is that most of the time we are dealing with perceptions caused by behaviours such as being inconsistent or disorganized or even demonstrating a lack of self-confidence.

Self-Help Tips to Increase Your Perceived Trustworthiness

- Learn to say exactly what you mean. Many people try to elaborate or explain or justify everything they say. Make your statements factual and impersonal, not opinions. Prepare for what you want to say and how you can deliver your key points succinctly.

- Don't embellish or try to oversell or stretch the truth. Be able to substantiate what you say and be realistic with what you commit to do. Failure to deliver on your commitments is a major contributor to whether you are perceived as trustworthy.

- Keep confidential information confidential. Don't spread rumours or talk behind someone's back.

- Take responsibility for your actions and don't try to blame others. Admit your mistakes and look for ways to correct them and repair any damage that may have been done. Learn from your mistakes and demonstrate what you have learned.

- Don't take credit for other people's work. If you are inappropriately given credit, stand up and tell others who deserves the real credit.

- Don't say things (such as "I'll take care of that") if you have no intention of following through or not say things to avoid conflict (such as not correcting people when you know they have the wrong information). Leaving people with the wrong impression or the wrong facts will eventually backfire.

- Don't withhold information that is important for the proper running of the business. Some people believe that information is power, and having that information gives them a feeling of importance. Make sure if you are withholding information that it is not information that your bosses, employees, and peers need to effectively and efficiently perform their work.

- Simple things you do can give the impression that you are not trustworthy—not returning phone calls, not sending information you promised to send, not following through on something others believe you promised to take care of. All of these little things can damage your relationship with others as well as give you an unwanted reputation for not being trustworthy.

Learns through Action: You are a quick learner and can understand how things work or what to do when shown new things or placed in unknown situations. You will try a variety of different fixes when dealing with problems, and you learn from what doesn't work. When you learn something new, you can apply that knowledge to other situations and new problems. You enjoy the challenge that comes from facing new problems or unfamiliar assignments and won't stop until you find a solution.

Most people are good at using solutions or techniques that they have learned or used in the past. Most people can generally solve problems they have solved previously. There are, however, significantly fewer people who have the ability to analyse and do things or solve problems they have never seen before. The ability to see new challenges, learn quickly, and apply that learning is a skill that is crucial in an environment that is ever changing. This skill requires abandoning what is currently known, looking at new things in new ways, taking risks, and setting new direction. During one of my assignments our leadership team was charged with implementing a new production system. When the new system was designed it became clear that we were not going to be able to get the required volume of parts based on the way the assembly line was designed. At that time all assembly lines were designed as moving conveyors, and in order for employees to complete their tasks they had to walk beside the assembly as it moved. Once that task was completed, the employees then had to return to the original starting point and try to catch up to the next moving assembly. After involving a group of employees and engineers, it was decided to redesign the assembly process so that the work area where the employees stood would move with the assembly, thus allowing the parts to be assembled in less time. This allowed for the required increase in volume that was needed. This redesign was subsequently used for all new assembly installations across the corporation.

Self-Help Tips to Develop Your Learning through Action Skill

- In many ways this skill is similar to dealing with uncertainty. It requires one to be comfortable dealing with the unknown, experimenting, breaking new ground, or learning new things. As in any new endeavour there is always fear of failure. Without failure we would never learn what is possible and what is not. A leader I worked with allowed his team to experiment with a new approach to installing pistons into an engine during the assembly process. Over the years this task had created a number of repetitive strain injuries on employees, and the leader was determined to find a better solution. He had challenged his employees, engineers, and supervisors to work together to find a solution. After many failed attempts, the team learned a tremendous amount about what would not work. After regrouping with this newfound knowledge, the team was able to develop a simple tool that could be used by the employee and eliminated any further injuries. The employees also agreed that this process improvement was better, and the solution was implemented quickly and without any resistance. Additionally, this activity could now be performed in less time, thus increasing the flow through the assembly process.

- When confronted with a new challenge or problem, the first step always starts with getting the best definition possible for the problem and then trying to figure out what caused it. Defining the problem starts by asking "why" several times to ensure that the root cause of the problem is identified. This up-front analysis of the situation will force you to not begin by trying to solve an ill-defined problem.

- When confronted with a complex problem or a new challenge that is difficult to understand, try to make the problem visual. Use a diagram or flowchart to show the elements contributing to the problem, the process flow, and how each element affects the outcome. This will help you identify what is working and what isn't.

- Look for patterns that are similar to other problems that you have solved and what similarities exist that might give you some insight as to the principles at play that will lead to a solution. During my time in engine assembly operations we had many engaged employees who came up with new ways of doing things that improved quality or reduced cost or reduced the risk of injuries. In our company we had seven engine assembly plants in operation at the time. One leader decided that we should document every assembly problem that we have as well as the solution and then create a database that could be shared and used by the other engine plants. This idea was developed and implemented, and it became a major source of information that allowed for the creation of common assembly processes across the company.

- Try to create quick tests or experiments that may give you immediate feedback as to what might work in solving the problem.

Don't stop at the first possible solution to a problem. Get people's input and suggestions and ask many questions. Answers to these questions may help to reformulate the problem and come up with a different solution.

Takes a Stand: You are comfortable working alone when required and are not afraid to be the lone voice providing a differing opinion. You will defend a position or champion a new idea and can be counted on when the situation heats up.

This competency involves becoming comfortable with conflict and confident enough to be the lone voice on an issue. It requires a high level of self-confidence and a strong ability to defend the rationale for your stand and to champion your position.

Self-Help Tips to Increase Your Ability to Take a Stand

- In order to be effective in taking a stand, you first have to believe in your position and feel comfortable that you are right and able to defend your position in the face of adversity. There will always be those who will criticize and say that a different position should be taken. To take a stand you have to be willing to take personal responsibility for mistakes and move forward. Criticism should not be the reason for not taking a stand.

- Be prepared to articulate your position and the rationale for taking it. Be prepared to consider the opposing view and willing to modify your position if you feel it requires modification.

- When you take a stand remember to focus only on the end point. Don't get locked into a specific way of getting there. Being flexible with how you get there may give you the leverage you need to get more people to support your position.

- Control your emotional reaction to push back. Look for the early signs of your emotional level increasing and pause or ask a question to allow yourself time to regain your composure.

- Be prepared to answer tough questions. In advance, try to think of the top ten questions you will most likely face and prepare short responses while you have the time to think it through. Practice the responses in front of others and get comfortable with your responses. Think of your responses as an additional opportunity to share a little more information about your position.

- There are times when questions are asked that shouldn't be answered. When confronted with one of those questions, try to turn it around and offer some suggestions of alternatives that could be considered. There are also times when people will not accept your answer to their question and will continue to argue and encourage you to continue in the dialogue. If possible, agree to disagree and suggest that the individual has obviously had different experiences than you and that you appreciated the opportunity to debate the issue.

- When considering whether you want to take a stand on an issue, be sure that the issue is important enough for you to stand alone and deal with the consequences.

Embraces Common Systems: You are someone who understands the value of common systems and the elimination of waste. You look for ways to reduce variances in work processes and continuously improve the quality of products and services to meet the needs of the customer. You are open to experimentation and changing processes if there is a potential to make the work flow more efficient, and you rely on data to drive your decision making.

The most effective way to ensure that your business is meeting your customers' expectations is by involving your employees in developing the systems and processes that achieve that objective and then documenting the system. Once the system is documented, everyone needs to be trained in the process and leadership must monitor to ensure that everyone follows the common system. An example of a common system that we used was a common quality-measuring process. This process allowed us to determine all the critical points that should be checked to ensure product quality and also allowed for a consistent way of performing the task as well as the frequency for making these checks. Without this common system, we learned that individuals will do what they believe to be the right thing but in doing so may overlook a critical dimension or perform the checks at a different frequency, which might put the quality of the product in jeopardy. If a quality problem did occur, using a common process allows for tracking where and when the problem occurred and quickly containing any product that could be suspect. There is often a misconception that common systems eliminate innovation and creativity. We have found the exact opposite. If people think they have a better idea, they have to present their idea to the team and get agreement that the idea is better. If agreed, the common system is modified, and everyone is then required to follow the improved process. We also learned that monitoring is usually required to ensure that everyone follows the new common system. Experience shows that leadership must demonstrate what is important and measure and monitor the behaviours to reinforce their importance.

Self-Help Tips to Develop Your Ability to Embrace Common Systems

- Take the time to learn the principles of a total integrated work system (read Dr. Deming, Dr. Juran, or Dr. Crosby's books—there are many others as well—on lean manufacturing and the seven forms of waste). A total integrated work system exists when all aspects of the production system are designed to produce a predetermined amount of parts, which may include machining lines, assembly processes, quality processes, maintenance processes to ensure equipment functions as designed, and appropriate staffing levels. In the engine-assembly plant that I worked at we designed an integrated production system to produce three thousand engines per day. In order to do that we had to decide what parts we were going to make and what parts we were going to buy. For the parts we made, we installed machining lines to produce enough components to support the assembly line assembling three thousand engines per day. We set up our tooling to support machining enough parts to support assembling three thousand engines per day. We developed a maintenance system that allowed access to the equipment to perform required preventive maintenance and still produce the required amount of parts to support assembling three thousand engines per day. For purchased parts we received enough parts from vendors at predetermined times during each day to support the build of three thousand engines per day. We also set up a shipping schedule that allowed us to ship three thousand engines per day to our various vehicle assembly plants (our customers).

- Consider what you do from the customer's vantage point, not yours. (Ask yourself, *If customers knew what I was doing would they agree that this work is added value, and would they be willing to pay for it?*)

- Be open to continuous improvement. Never be satisfied with the status quo, and strive for producing zero product defects and services that the customer wants. Engage everyone in developing your work processes and find ways to perform tasks in the most effective and efficient ways and look for ways to eliminate waste.

Problem Solving: When problems arise, you look for the root causes and seek permanent solutions to deal with the symptoms. You know how to use multiple methods to analyse problems and consider all alternatives when looking for resources appropriate to the situation. Once you've found a solution and implemented it, follow up to ensure that it has actually resolved the problem long term and make adjustments as necessary.

Most people believe that they are smart enough to solve problems effectively, but most don't do it right. Most people don't spend enough time defining the actual problem, and they tend to solve a way of dealing with a symptom. Some people overanalyse and never get to the point of actually trying a solution. But most of all people in general rely too much on themselves to try to solve a problem instead of pulling together a group of people with different knowledge and experiences and increasing the likelihood of actually solving the root cause of the problem.

Self-Help Tips to Improve Your Problem-Solving Skill

- Resist the temptation to jump into action before you have had a chance to analyse and define the problem. Ask "why" five times to increase the likelihood of actually defining the real problem that needs solving.

- Resist the impatience of people who tend to always want to take control and jump to a conclusion.

- Be careful not to use the same solution for all problems. One solution may have worked on one problem, but you need to analyse and define the problem clearly before you try to use a solution that previously worked. Also, don't rely solely on your own history to resolve a problem—don't hesitate to ask others for their input and advice.

- Unless the consequences of a decision can create irreparable damage, be careful not to spend all of your time in analysis mode. You will never have all the data or information to make a perfect decision 100 percent of the time. (Some people fall into this trap either because they are perfectionists and always want to make the perfect decision or because they fear negative consequences from making the wrong decision.) When analysing, look at trends and patterns, identify several possible alternatives, and select the one that you or the team believes has the highest likelihood of success. If possible, try an experiment first to see if you get the results you expect.

- Complex problems are most difficult to deal with as there tends to be many variables and interrelationships. When confronted with a complex problem, use tools such as flowcharts, pictures, data trends, etc., to help visualize the relationship of each element to each other and the possible contribution to the real problem.

- As in most other decision situations, it is critically important to be organized and disciplined in methods used to analyse the situation. If necessary, create checklists or procedures to follow to ensure the rigor is present in your analysis.

Organizing/Planning/Time Management: You provide structure and order to a mass of information so that it may be used effectively and efficiently. You possess the ability to coordinate multiple activities to accomplish a goal and arrange it so that all necessary resources are used to accomplish a task. You understand the needs of the business and can effectively set objectives to meet those needs. You break down the objectives into time-based activities and can assign responsibilities to the appropriate people to ensure accomplishment. You also know when it's necessary to make adjustments to the plan and are always monitoring the performance of activities to ensure the objective is met on time.

Whoever has enough time? There are so many things to do and not enough time to do all of them. There is a finite amount of resources and infinite needs. All of us have more to do than we can get to. The higher up you are in an organization, the more people you manage, the more areas of responsibility you have, the more you have to do and the less amount of time you have to do it. No one can do it all! You have to set priorities. You have to delegate. And you have to manage your time well to survive and prosper.

It is easier to get things done when everyone is pulling in the same direction. It is easier to perform when you have all the tools and resources you need. It is easier to get things done when everyone you need is supportive and pulling for you. Unless you prefer doing things the hard way, time needs to be spent planning and organizing.

Self-Help Tips to Help Build Your Skill in Organizing, Planning, and Managing Your Time

- Build a plan for completing the work. Know what you want to accomplish; what needs to be done to accomplish the task; who controls the resources needed (people, funds, tools, materials, support); who will benefit from the work; and who will lose from the work. Write out the sequence of steps that need to be followed along with who will do them and the prescribed timeline. The plan should be reviewed at regular intervals, and if a step is off track, a recovery plan should be put in place to meet the original deadline established for meeting the goal.

- Share your goal and plan with people you need to support you. Create a sense of ownership by asking for their input and figuring out how they, too, will win by providing their support.

- Find coworkers who are better at organizing and time management than you. Watch what they do and compare it to what you typically do. Ask for assistance and try to increase doing the things that they do to organize and manage their time. Ask for feedback from people who have commented on your organizing and time-management skills and ask what you could do differently.

- Plan your time and manage against it. Spend your time on activities that require your skills and abilities. Figure out what are the largest time wasters for you and consider ways to reduce them. Try to batch similar activities and minimize redundancy and use avenues such as e-mail and voice mail for routine matters. Use your time for matters that are important.

- Do a little planning and delegate those things that do not require your skills or don't have to be done by you, especially activities that are time consuming. If you have a complex or multitask project to do, break the project into a series of tasks that make up the whole and assign responsibilities based on the skill level of your staff or other members of your team.

- For managers, this may also be a great opportunity to develop employees who you believe have the skill but have never been tested. Research shows that empowered people work longer and harder. People like to have control over their work, determine how to do it, and have the authority to make decisions. Give employees as many of the tasks as possible along with the authority to make decisions within well-defined boundaries. Stay in touch and offer support, especially to your weakest links, but don't do the work for them. Let them learn and fail if necessary, and help them learn from their mistakes.

- Often we are asked to do more than we can handle. If what you are being asked to do does not require your skills and abilities or is not a priority for the business or, in the case of managers, their employees, you need to consider saying "no." When it is necessary to say no it should be done constructively. Explain why your time cannot be used to fulfill the request. Explain that your skills are not needed to complete the request. Explain that we should not be using our limited business resources and time on an activity that has not been defined as a priority for the business or our employees.

- Get in the habit of sharing the successes with the people who helped achieve the goal and with those who supported you. Remember, do not celebrate or provide positive reinforcement or feedback unless you can clearly identify what behaviour the individual exhibited that you want to see again tomorrow! This will make it easier to go back to people the next time you need their help, support, or involvement.

Personal Development: You're committed to improving yourself and actively pursue development of the skills necessary for future career opportunities. You look to understand your strengths and weaknesses and strive to compensate for or develop areas of weakness. You recognize the importance of lifelong learning.

I hope we can all agree that those who continuously learn and grow and, in general, better themselves are more likely to be successful in their careers than those who don't. We all have skills that are considered our strengths, but we also all have skills that are either underdeveloped or overused. Remaining stagnant and not focusing on our own development will not prepare us for the needs of the future.

Not listening to feedback or not doing anything about known areas of weakness will likely have a negative impact on your career.

Self-Help Tips for Personal Development

- It all starts by getting to know yourself better than anyone else. Search out feedback from all sources—managers, coworkers, employees, customers, suppliers, or even friends. Have them help you identify what you do well, what you do poorly, what skills you lack, and what skills you overuse. Find out what others think you should keep doing, stop doing, or start doing. Use some of the many available self-assessment tools to get a better understanding of you and your natural tendencies.

- Learn what skills are important to be successful in your current role and for those roles you aspire to reach. Do an assessment of your skills against the skills needed for those roles and develop a plan to develop in those critical areas. Seek the assistance of your manager and, if necessary, seek the help of a personal coach.

- Identify people who would benefit from being coached by you in one of your areas of strength and ask them to coach you in one of their areas of strength that you need help with.

- If you have areas of weakness you may not always be able to develop them into a strength. It may be possible for you to at least focus on getting that skill to an acceptable level or to find other ways to compensate for the area of weakness. Some skills can only be improved by being involved in an assignment or project. Look for support from your manager to identify opportunities that would help you to develop that skill or competency.

- Ask someone you consider to have a strength in a competency that you want to develop to monitor you and provide you with ongoing feedback and help as you work to improve in that area. Until you have the confidence that you have developed a skill that was previously considered weak, avoid taking on assignments alone that could leave you vulnerable to getting in trouble.

- Don't be afraid to ask for help and to show others that you are trying to improve in areas that are important. Generally, others will provide assistance if they believe that you are serious about your development and are willing to try to improve.

Technical Skills: You have the technical knowledge and skills necessary to perform at a high level of competence and are not afraid to try new technologies.

All functional areas have some technologies that are designed specifically for their type of work. Performing work within the function generally requires a high level of technical and functional knowledge. Developing the technical skills to become proficient makes you an asset to the organization. Having marginal skills makes you a liability. Some examples of the type of technical skills we are referring to may include getting the recognized engineering certification and not just an engineering degree; becoming certified as a "master" in quality problem solving; learning to use the latest versions of the software used by your company and its application to your function; joining an external group that deals with keeping everyone in your function up to date in new developments such as engineering societies or human resource groups or safety standards groups.

Self-Help Tips to Increase Technical Skills

- Ask for help from the pros and demonstrate a true interest in learning.

- Ask others in your function what skills and knowledge are most critical to learn and how they learned them. Follow the path suggested and ask if they would tutor you.

- Become a member of a technical association that deals in technologies affecting your business. Look for experts with whom you can build a personal relationship and ask them to tutor you.

- Take courses, read books and articles, and attend conferences where new technologies are shown.

- Find out what sources are used to introduce new technologies, such as magazines or books or quarterly reports, and subscribe.

- Select a technology and practice using it for new applications either at work or at home. Become proficient and then select a different technology.

I think it's important to reiterate that these basics are not used to decide who should climb up the business ladder; but rather they are the personality traits and characteristics that make a good impression on management and open the door for advancement consideration. If you have these basics mastered, business leaders are more willing and able to see whether or not you have the competencies and skills required for different positions or categories.

In the next few chapters, we'll learn what competencies are most associated with success within each of the three categories of career paths. Although the competencies identified under each category are considered the main differentiators, you will note that many of the competencies identified in the individual contributor role also have applicability to the manager or even the executive role. Although these competencies remain important as a person progresses into the managerial structure, other competencies begin to play a more important role in defining success in their categories. I believe this will become clearer as you read through the next three chapters.

Chapter 3

Individual Contributor Role

An individual contributor is an individual who does not supervise or manage others but instead performs specific tasks or duties or has specialized skills and responsibilities. These roles tend to be held by individuals who are subject-matter experts or have specialty interests or skills and whose knowledge is crucial to the success of the business. These individuals tend to be relied on to provide knowledge or direction on specific topics or processes. These individuals get the job done. To be successful in this career category, individual contributors are generally recognized for their specialty knowledge, intelligence, problem-solving capability, and ability to get results.

The following are the most significant competencies associated with performance success in an individual contributor role. If this describes you, there is a strong possibility you would succeed in this type of career path.

Process Development: You can simplify complex processes to improve work flow efficiency and use process improvements and synergy to use fewer resources. You're an expert at breaking activities down into smaller, simple tasks and then combining them to optimize work flows.

All things happen in a given sequence even if the sequence is not known. Actions and reactions are generally predictable, and the best way to get the highest quality at the lowest cost and use the fewest resources is to develop a standardized process and follow it rigorously. Those that do not follow predictable processes end up dealing with variation in their products or services and eventually dissatisfied customers.

Self-Help Tips to Increase Your Process-Development Skill

- Start by defining what needs to be accomplished and what resources are needed. Identify what needs to be done and in what order to meet the accomplishment. Try to lay out the work flow to visually show what tasks are necessary in what sequence. Show what resources are needed for each task. If possible use a team to analyse the details of the flowchart to see if the sequence makes sense or if improvements can be made. Involve people who have performed this work or similar work who can help identify potential problems or ways to improve the flow or use fewer resources.

- Revise the plan to incorporate the input from the team and develop a standardized process. Review the final process with those people who will be required to use it to get their buy in, and then train everyone in the new process.

- Put measures in place to ensure that the process is followed by everyone. If some believe that they have a way to improve the process, require them to outline their proposed change to all affected people and get their agreement that the change is in fact an enhancement. At this point the process should be revised, everyone should be retrained, and measures must be put in place to ensure that everyone is following the new and improved process.

Technically Smart: You have a capacity for learning technical things quickly and can develop technical skills and knowledge for use in new applications. You have a strong understanding for how things work.

Technology is emerging at faster speeds than at any other time in our history. It is changing how we communicate, how we perform work, and how we interact with customers and suppliers. New learnings are being shared at lightning speed through the use of the Internet. Keeping up with technology is crucial to any business's long-term survival as speed and competition increases.

Self-Help Tips to Increase Your Technical Knowledge

- Become a member of a technical association that deals in technologies affecting your business. Look for experts with whom you can build a personal relationship and ask them to tutor you.

- Take courses, read books and articles, and attend conferences where new technologies are shown.

- Find out what sources are used to introduce new technologies, such as magazines or books or quarterly reports, and subscribe.

- Select a technology and practice using it for new applications either at work or at home. Become proficient, and then select a different technology.

Shrewd: You can relate effectively to all levels of the organization, and you have both good judgment and tact. You build rapport with key people both inside and outside the organization and are capable of diffusing tension in high-stress situations.

Getting along with different types of people is a characteristic that will help anyone in the business world. Your ability to build relationships can have a lasting positive impact on your ability to get things done. Being shrewd is about not reacting with emotion to others when you first meet them but waiting to see what interpersonal approach is best suited for this individual. Being shrewd is about using the right interpersonal skill and approach at the right time.

Self-Help Tips to Increase Your Understanding and Effectiveness in Being Shrewd

- We live in a world full of diversity, and by that we mean diverse in every way. Not only do we mean differences in age, race, gender, creed, or national origin, but we also mean personality, composure, emotion, motivation level, or even communication skills or intelligence. To understand people, you need to look and listen to what people do and say when you first meet them. What is important to them can be observed in what they emphasize when they talk. What style do they exhibit when they interact with others? For example, do they take control and dominate; do they withdraw and listen; do they speak loudly or softly? Listen for those things that they are passionate or emotional about and try to understand what they value.

- Once you have some knowledge of a person's interaction style you can then use a similar complementary style to build your relationship around this first impression. Getting along with people helps when business transactions need to be made as the focus is only on the transaction and not on the differences in style or approach.

- When trying to build a reputation for getting along with everyone, you need to look in the mirror and reflect on your own style to see if you are creating barriers or walls that will negate your ability to get along with others. Do you come across as overconfident or arrogant? Do you take time to interact with people and get to know them as a person? Are you good at listening to others, or do you have a tendency to interrupt or cut people off? Do you react abruptly when you disagree with someone? All of these behaviours can become roadblocks to people wanting to build a relationship or even get along with you.

- People who are highly skilled at using interpersonal skills are great listeners. They make others feel comfortable, important, and that they matter. Don't interrupt people when they are talking; don't look at your watch (which indicates you are really not interested in what they have to say); ask clarifying questions; don't judge; and seek to understand what you are being told.

- Just as important as listening is managing your nonverbal communications. Smile and make the person feel comfortable. Be relaxed and attentive, and maintain eye contact during the conversation. Acknowledge that you are listening while the other person is speaking by giving a little nod. Try not to appear impatient or disinterested.

If you are an introvert or are generally shy and uncomfortable meeting new people, you will have to overcome those feelings to develop in this area. Try practicing meeting new people outside the workplace. Try different approaches and see which one makes you feel most comfortable and puts the other person at ease. Try starting the conversation by asking a question, and then listen and maintain eye contact. The best way to overcome these feelings or at least neutralize them is to practice the behaviours that make you appear extroverted.

To be highly efficient and effective in an individual contributor role you need to have a well-developed set of most or all of these competencies and have the ability to develop further in areas that are underdeveloped or untested. To be truly successful in an individual contributor role individuals must embrace this category and be focused on being the best they can be based on their skill set and interests.

Promotional Indicators

Many people in an individual contributor role have career aspirations to move into a higher level within the management ranks. If you are interested in being considered for a manager role inside your organization there are two competencies that are thought to be strong indicators of promotional consideration: *perseverance* and *taking action*. Look for opportunities that demonstrate that you are proficient and have a high level of skill especially in these competencies.

Perseverance: You will keep working or pursuing solutions with drive and energy until the goal is accomplished. You will not give up when faced with setbacks or when confronted with resistance.

This skill is needed when you get push back from others when you present your ideas or when you tried something and it did not go right or as well as you expected. Perseverance is not only about not giving up; it is also about trying different approaches or alternatives to accomplish a task or a goal. Some people do not persevere because they fear failure and the negativity associated with it or they fear rejection or are not comfortable taking a stand in pursuit of something they believe in that is worthwhile to the business.

Self-Help Tips to Develop Your Skill in Persevering

- If what you tried the first time does not work or does not give you the results you expect, try a new approach or a different alternative. It is highly unlikely that doing the same thing again will produce a different result. Early in my career I had a belief that if you were in a position of power others would listen to you or do what you say. Experience has taught me that sending an e-mail or a letter may not get the response from someone that you are looking for. Sometimes you may have to make a presentation or arrange a face-to-face discussion to get others to do what you want them to do. Sometimes having the opportunity to listen to the reasons or logic behind someone's resistance may cause you to look at what you are asking in a different light or give you an opportunity to explain your view firsthand.

- When confronted with resistance, ask others for their feedback, ideas, or input to get a better outcome. Stay focused on the goal and reinforce how a positive outcome would be beneficial for the business.

- Start the second or third attempt in a reasonable period of time after the first attempt—don't put it off. Don't get caught against time lines or you may be forced to give up on your idea.

- When dealing with resistance after the first attempt fails, be prepared with data and your business case to support your continuing effort and prepare yourself to answer the tough questions. Be confident and forceful if you believe in your idea and that it is worth doing.

- Only take on those issues that are really important. You can't persevere on everything, and you could develop a reputation for just being argumentative and not being able to deliver results. Pick your battles. Make sure you are pushing the right set of priorities.

Takes Action: You are not someone who will spend days or weeks discussing everything and examining every last possibility to the point where nothing ever happens. You act quickly on things that are challenging, and you enjoy hard work. You approach challenges with a high level of energy and will take action after basic planning because you are focused on the "doing" and "trying" to discover solutions that work rather than just finding a theoretical solution.

Every organization needs speed and the ability to react quickly to changing forces in the market. A propensity toward action is always favoured over inaction, because those who hesitate are usually overtaken by those who don't. There are generally three areas where inaction comes from: procrastination, risk aversion, or perfectionism. All of these cause delays and prevent others from taking quick timely action. I once worked for a leader who wanted data collected and analysed for every decision he was asked to make. In several cases after being presented with the requested data he would ask for more data to support the decision; he would even ask for data to support *not* taking action. I later came to learn that whenever this leader made a decision he would always be challenged by his director and usually he would be criticized for making a change when things "weren't broken." This was at the root of his resistance to support changes, but it was having another effect. Our customer perceived us as being unresponsive and out of touch with what was happening outside our company.

Self-Help Tips to Increase Your Ability to Take Action

- Taking action generally starts with having the confidence to move forward. If you are not comfortable with your level of confidence, you need to begin by identifying your strengths and your weaknesses and then take a course or get a coach and try to build your strength and confidence in one area at a time. When confronted with a decision to take action or not, try to use those areas of strength to move you toward taking action.

- If you are a procrastinator you will already have experienced missing a deadline or running out of time to complete a task or not performing an activity or task at an acceptable level. *Start earlier.* When given an assignment or project, do some of it immediately after being assigned. Break the remaining activities into smaller pieces and commit to doing some of it every day and plan to have it completed ahead of your deadline.

- Perfectionists are in the same league as those that are committed to endless analysis. In the real world there usually isn't enough time to wait for a perfect solution or opportunities will be missed. Try to make more decisions with less data over time and see what impact takes place when you move to action without a perfect solution or a solution based on some data. You have to move your thinking from "perfect every time" to "everything can be improved" and accept that the process of continuous improvement will move you closer and closer to perfection in time. And in the meantime you haven't let opportunities go by due to inaction.

- Some people are just uncomfortable with the idea that they might make a mistake, and therefore they become unwilling to take a risk. They believe that if they don't make decisions or take action, then they can't be blamed for making mistakes. These individuals are afraid of how they will be viewed and what the repercussions will be for failure. Treat mistakes and failures as opportunities to learn. Start small so that any mistake or error made will be minor and you can recover quickly. Break tasks into smaller activities and build up your confidence. When confronted with a mistake, take the time to debrief and see what could be done differently next time to get a better outcome. Over time, increase your level of risk taking and you will learn to take calculated risks.

Setting the Stage for a Manager's Role

Individual contributors who have a career interest in moving into the management ranks need to also be aware that there are additional competencies required for effective performance in a manager's role.

Although it may be difficult at times to use these competencies when performing in an individual contributor role, you need to look for opportunities to develop them or demonstrate that you have them. Although situations may arise when you have the opportunity to use one of these competencies, the fact that you were able to effectively use the competency when you did not have supervisory control over the people or the situation also shows your ability to influence others. As you are considered for positions in the management structure, demonstrating proficiency in these areas will hold you in good stead. The competencies that are necessary for effective performance in a manager's role should begin to evolve and become visible while in an individual contributors role include the following.

Motivates Others: Your motivation doesn't stop with yourself. You create enthusiasm in others, and doing so compels their commitment to the goals of the organization. You use empowerment to challenge others and get their best efforts and create a sense of ownership in others for accomplishing the task at hand. You make all feel like valued members of the team and that what they do is important. Most of us understand that we can accomplish more, deal with more stress, or more deeply dedicate ourselves to something when we feel motivated. It is critical to understand that only a small percentage of the population are self-motivated. For the others, motivation tends to flow from the work environment and how they feel they are treated. Is there a high level of trust in your company? Do you feel respected? Do your opinions matter? Do you feel valued and an important part of the business? Although we all want to feel motivated, each individual may be motivated by different things. A good manager will learn what motivates each individual and use that knowledge in dealing with that employee.

Self-Help Tips to Increase Your Effectiveness in Motivating Others

- There are some basic things that we do that matter to people, and these things are no different than the things that matter to you. When someone does something that you value, say "thank you." Tell people that what they do is important and show them how what they do impacts the company. Show a personal interest in all employees and demonstrate an interest in their career and their development. Understand what each employee's interests are and attempt to provide opportunities that are in line with his or her interests.

- Involve employees in setting reasonable goals for their work and use goals as an opportunity to measure their performance and provide them positive feedback. Setting goals should involve a level of challenge that requires the individual to stretch, but the goal should be achievable.

- Use the "language" (or phrases and terms) that individuals speak to make them open up and feel more at ease. This is particularly important when dealing across generational lines and is generally seen as a sign of respect. When employees speak, look for clues as to what motivates or excites them. Look for changes in their tone of voice or passionate stories or signs that give you insight into their values. This knowledge is valuable when you are looking for ways to motivate this person.

- Delegation is important in motivating people if you allow them to determine the way they will achieve their targets. Involve people in the goals of their total work area and include them in the team successes and in debriefing sessions about team failures where learning will take place. Also allow employees to use their full skill set and help them develop new ones.

Command and Control: You naturally take over the lead in a crisis or adversarial situation and do so capably. You're not afraid to take a tough stand and force debate, and you're energized by challenges.

Leading is exciting and personally rewarding, but it also opens one up to challenge. When put in charge of a major project team or a crisis situation, the challenge becomes getting others to follow and believe in the direction you are taking them. In these situations, the leader's role is to set goals, assign responsibilities, measure performance, deal with pressures and roadblocks, manage emotions, be the team's role model, make tough decisions on things impacting the assignment, align team members and resources, and inspire action.

In my time heading the HRM activity I was exposed to a number of situations involving dealing with significant change. One situation involved making major modifications to our benefit plans, which had become excessive compared to our competitors. And the additional cost was weighing heavily on our balance sheet. The situation required making several tough decisions that were going to affect all employees, including the members of my team. I decided that I needed to share the cost information that I had with my team members and show them how these costs were impacting our balance sheet. I allowed them to vent (which I suspected would be their immediate reaction) and then asked them to go away and think about what I shared with them and to provide me their input on how we should deal with the situation. When we reconvened, the team individually and collectively acknowledged that we needed to make some changes, but everyone was concerned about the reaction we would receive from the workforce. At this point, I acknowledged their concern and committed that collectively we would work to help everyone understand the situation as well as we did so that they would at least have an understanding of why the changes were being made. The team then began to work at identifying where changes needed to be made. Collectively we developed a package that met our cost-reduction objective and a communication package to explain the actual changes and why the changes were being made.

Self-Help Tips to Build Your Skill in Command and Control

- To be effective as a leader one needs to demonstrate confidence in oneself. If you cannot be confident in yourself, you can't expect that others will. Have a strong voice, be a great listener, portray a positive attitude, and be confident in your ability to take advice from other.

- Making tough decisions and defending them is difficult, so practice by thinking through in advance a summary of what your decision is and why you believe it is the right one. You need to be confident enough to take a stand, so if you are shaky about your position, ask others whom you respect to validate your position.

- When leading a team it is important to remember that team members have a lot to contribute. Stay focused on the team goals and outcomes and support the team by letting them decide how to get there. It is critical in this situation to lay out any parameters or boundaries in advance of empowering the team.

- Learn to recognize how you show your emotions. In a leadership role, if you show that you are not in control of your emotions, others will think that you are having difficulty leading or you lack confidence in your direction. If you are uncomfortable in a situation, buy time by asking questions or ask others' opinions or simply find a way to leave until you regain your composure.

- When dealing with confrontation in any lead role you have to become a good listener and stay objective. When in this situation let other people talk as long as they are willing to do so and then ask if they have anything else to add. Try to restate their key points and ask them to confirm your understanding. Tell the person what you agree with and then take each point and provide your response or suggest that more information is needed and that it should be taken off line. Keep the issue about facts and data rather than emotion or opinion.

- When dealing in a crisis situation, generally time is the enemy. Gather all information that is readily available or can be gathered in a reasonable amount of time. Take the information and with the help of others try to make the best sense possible of the situation, get opinions from others, and then make your decision. Have someone prepare for the worst possible outcome and put a continuous communication process in place to be able to modify the direction on a moment's notice. Try to stay cool and calm and in control.

- Look for opportunities to lead such as a highly visible project or even volunteer outside the organization. Be prepared to take the heat and defend your decisions. Also be a good listener for team member input, but remember to stay in control. When the project is complete or a major aspect is complete, take the time to debrief and to learn what went well and what didn't and look for input as to what could be done different next time to improve the outcome.

Manages Conflict: While many people shy away from conflict and make an effort to avoid it, you see conflict as an opportunity for improvement. You're an effective listener and are able to quickly understand underlying issues. You manage conflicts among people by finding the common ground and looking for the win-win solution to create postdispute cooperation.

In today's work environments the level of stress has never been higher. There is pressure to do things better, faster, and with fewer resources in order to stay ahead of the competition globally. With these added stressors comes greater conflict as individuals try to fight for resources or for limited promotional opportunities or to protect their turf or even their job. Unresolved conflict has the effect of people focusing on the conflict issue and not on what is best for the business, so it is critically important for conflict to be resolved quickly and fairly. In my role as director of HR I found myself in the middle of a number of conflicts among leaders who were all trying to do what they thought was the best thing. One situation I dealt with involved a conflict over how resources were going to be split between operations in Canada versus the United States. In this situation I gathered the individuals responsible for these allocations and conducted a face-to-face meeting. The first thing we did was define the problem we had with the resource allocation decision and then proceeded to show how the decision was going to impact the operations in Canada. The impact ultimately would be felt by the United States as the results from Canadian operations were combined with those from the United States and the same individuals who made the decision on resources would ultimately have to explain the performance results in Canada. After much discussion, we agreed to put together a business case showing what level of resources we could attain without negatively affecting Canadian operational performance. Once submitted, the business case was ultimately approved.

Self-Help Tips to Increase Effectiveness in Managing Conflict

- One of the best ways to manage conflict is to prevent it in the first place. The most effective way of preventing conflict is to build relationships that will lead to a better understanding of how others are feeling and a general feeling of being respected. When you have good relationships at work it leads to both individuals focusing on the issue at hand and finding win-win solutions.

- Be aware of how you come across to others in your dialogue. Avoid being insensitive and loud or abusive in your language. Demonstrate respect for others, and challenge issues and not people. Try not to assess blame and focus on defining the problem versus providing a solution to an ill-defined situation. If you find that someone has done something that created a problem, be tactful in dealing with the issue and allow the individual the opportunity to suggest a potential solution and save face in the process.

- Learn to listen and not react. When confronted with individuals who are reacting emotionally to a situation, try to filter through their emotions and understand the issue. Ask clarifying questions to ensure that you have a firm understanding of the issue behind the emotion. Repeat back what you believe you heard was the issue and try to get the individual to focus on the issue and what could be done to resolve the situation. If necessary offer to help or intervene. If the individual has a lot of pent-up emotion and cannot focus on the issue at hand, ask him or her to do something else and regain his or her composure and be willing to discuss the situation at a later time.

- Even in conflict situations there is some agreement between the individuals. When confronted with conflict, try to break the issue into smaller components and attempt to find parts that you are in agreement with. Doing this will help to minimize the size of the problem, reduce the emotion, and make the issue more manageable to resolve.

There will be times when conflict cannot be resolved between two parties. When confronted with this situation, agree to disagree, try to agree on the problem definition, and try to agree to bring a third party into the discussion to mediate or arbitrate the situation. If this option is used it is important that the individuals agree in advance that they are prepared to live with the outcome of the situation.

- Another form of conflict involves discussion between managers and employees when performance problems exist. These tend to be the most difficult situations for managers to deal with, and more often than not, because of that they avoid the discussion or wait until it becomes unsolvable. Like all other management situations, it all starts by laying out the facts. Employees need to know how their performance is perceived at the time it is noted. Waiting until an annual performance review to tell an employee that their performance is subpar isn't fair to the employee or to the company. Give the employee an opportunity to think about what you have shared and ask them to meet again after they have had a chance to digest the news. When you reconvene, you need to be clear on your expectations of the employee and give him or her a chance to offer suggestions on how they can improve. If you agree, be prepared to support the employee with training or relearning, but don't lower your expectations. If the individual has fully engaged in coming up with a plan to improve his or her performance, set a timeframe for the improvement to take place. Also have regular reviews to ensure that progress is being made and that the employee is committed to the plan. Hopefully this will bring about a positive change in the employees performance, but if it doesn't, you will need to cut your losses by separating the individual. This solution is fair to the company and allows the individual to recompose and start fresh in a new career or company.

Effective Communicator: You are rarely at a loss for words and are able to help others understand their role and how they fit into the business.

You provide timely information to people that assists them in efficiently performing their jobs and making good decisions; you provide business information to help everyone know how the business is performing and how they can personally affect change.

Being able to effectively communicate with others is in the lowest quadrant of developed skills for the population in general and is one of the most critical ones in getting others to have the right information or direction to be able to perform effectively. When you communicate effectively, people are more aligned and more motivated and things just go better!

A leader I was coaching had received feedback from a survey that she was not sharing information with her staff. In one of our coaching sessions she confided in me that she was devastated by this feedback as she felt she was doing a good job at communicating with her staff. As I probed a little deeper I learned that she was trying to be sensitive to how busy her people were so she was filtering out information that wasn't directly related to their jobs. She also reduced the frequency of the meetings she was having with her employees with the intent of freeing them up to have more time to complete their busy assignments. In debriefing the situation with her she came to understand that the feedback she was receiving was that employees no longer had enough information to be able to have an understanding of how what they were doing was impacting the business and also that the information she was sharing was generally too late and already had an impact on their daily activities. Through our coaching sessions this leader changed her approach to communicating with her staff and actually reversed what she was doing previously. Any information that she had that directly affected her employees was communicated immediately and not held for the next meeting. Overall business performance was shared as a regular part of her communication meetings. The meetings were also reformatted so that employees were able to understand how their performance impacted the business. The communications became two-way, whereby employees were given the opportunity to express what they thought they could do to help improve the performance of the business.

Self-Help Tips to Become a More Effective Communicator

- Take the time to plan your communications. Figure out who needs what information to do their job and by when. If you expect others to make decisions on their job, what information should they have to be able to make the best decisions possible? When you communicate in advance, employees have what they need up front to proceed and they don't have to wait to talk to you or ask questions to get the clarity they need to move forward. If you are uncertain about what information employees need, ask them!

- When you provide only enough information for individuals to do their piece of a larger task, they will not understand the overall picture and therefore will not be able to know if their piece fits or not. It is also very disempowering to only know a part of the picture; thus employees will not be motivated. Give employees enough information to know what the whole team is trying to accomplish, why, and by when ... and then get out of the way.

- Keep everyone involved and informed on the progress of the group. Let them feel that they are part of something bigger than their own task and let them "own" the responsibility for sharing in the team meeting its goal. When things are not going as planned, let everyone know the status and ask for everyone's opinion of how the team can get back on track.

- If communicating is an issue for you, take the time to develop a list of what information is needed by whom and when. Refer to your checklist at set time intervals and ensure you make communicating information a priority.

If you are in an individual contributor role and your interests lie in becoming a manager, you need to take the initiative to learn the competencies that are related to performance success for that category and then dedicate to develop the skills and competencies necessary to excel *while at the same time trying to be the best you can be in your current role.* If you simply focus on developing your competencies for a manager role and do not put forth your best effort in your current role, there is a high probability that you will be perceived as having a negative attitude being solely interested in your career and not the impact your actions have on the business. The best approach is to develop the competencies for the category of interest and then look for opportunities to show that you possess the other competencies when opportunities present themselves.

Chapter 4

Manager Role

A manager is an individual who supervises or manages others in accomplishing work for a specific part of the business. In these positions the organization looks for people who have the ability to manage others, develop teams, and get the most out of others while being able to channel those efforts into the business goals and priorities. To be successful in this category a manager is generally recognized for the ability to plan, coordinate teams, motivate and engage people, use the skills of others to accomplish organizational goals, and drive accountability into the business.

In addition to the competencies identified in the previous chapter (motivates others, command and control, manages conflict, and effective communicator) the following competencies have been most associated with successful performance in a manager of people career category. If this describes you, there is a strong possibility you would succeed in this type of career path.

Manages Work: When working with others, you set clear objectives to be met, measure and assign responsibilities, and effectively follow up to monitor work progress and assist in removing roadblocks. You help develop recovery plans when tasks are not on time to ensure that the overall time line for the work is maintained.

This skill works in combination with the skills of being results-oriented and dealing with direct reports. The combination of these competencies deal with the skill of holding people accountable.

In today's economic environment most companies find that for their business to be successful they have to have their employees involved in making it as effective and efficient as possible. To achieve this requires managers who excel at confronting direct reports, being consistent, focusing on performance gaps, pitching in to help each person succeed, and being sensitive to how people feel. But if the effort fails, taking timely but compassionate action to separate the person from the company is required and is the ultimate test of managerial courage.

Most people like to have goals to measure themselves against a standard. They like the challenge of seeing who can perform the best work. They want goals to be realistic but stretching. Goals can make things more fair, an equitable way of measuring one person against another. People find it motivating to be part of the goal-setting process. This is all true if the goals and the measurements are used as opportunities for positive reinforcement!

Producing results means consistently meeting goals and objectives. Achieving results requires pushing yourself and others to achieve stretch goals. It means staying focused on the goal and acting and talking like you care about the bottom line.

Self-Help Tips to Increase Your Effectiveness in Managing Work

- For any business to prosper you need to identify what is critical to the business; what goals need to be achieved for the business to move forward; and what things have to get done to achieve the goals of the business. Answering these questions will provide the guidance necessary for the organization to set the direction and the goals for the business.

- Most people work better when they have a set of goals and objectives to meet and a standard that everyone agrees with to measure accomplishments against. Most people like stretch goals, especially if they are part of the process in setting them. People need to know how they will be measured and what the rewards/consequences are for exceeding, achieving, or missing the goals.

- Where it is appropriate, visually track progress toward goals over time. Consider displaying the tracking process as a reminder of the need to constantly focus on the goals. Feedback is important, as it reinforces that what people are working on is important. It also gives them an opportunity to course-correct if necessary to help them achieve the goals. Finally it is an opportunity to provide positive reinforcement that energizes people and helps them drive toward the finish line.

- Delivering bad news to people face to face has consistently been identified as the hardest and most hated tasks that managers have to do. It is tough to be the bearer of bad news. Emotions and defensiveness may flare up. The consequences could be severe. Managers may have to defend their actions outside the organization. The bottom line, though, is that it is cruel not to deliver honest performance feedback to individuals and at least give them a chance to improve before there are serious consequences.

Management Confidence: You understand what's important to senior leaders and you've mastered the art of speaking the language that gets the attention of senior leaders. You're confident and comfortable with higher management levels and can present information to senior leaders in a manner that is appropriate and meets their needs.

Interacting with members of higher-level management is difficult. They obviously have some strengths that allowed them to progress into their current role, they ask tough questions and want answers, and they have little time. There may also be a tendency for them to challenge you just to see how you handle it, and most have little sympathy about how they make you feel. Being able to perform and excel in this environment requires a high level of self-confidence and discipline.

Self-Help Tips to Increase Your Confidence Level when Dealing with Higher-Level Managers

- It is normal to feel nervous or anxious when performing around higher-level managers. The challenge is not to let these feelings prevent you from performing at your highest level. If you are feeling anxious or nervous, slow down, take a deep breath, and try to regain your composure. Don't forget that each of these managers has been in your shoes before, and keep in mind that you probably know more about the subject matter than anyone else in the room. So exhibit confidence in having this knowledge.

- Plan in advance what could go wrong and what questions you could be asked and prepare how you will react and respond. If possible, do a dry run and practice your presentation until you feel confident that you know the material.

- Ask others how these managers think and for any tips that should be prepared for this audience.

- Look for opportunities to network and develop relationships with higher-level managers. Finding out that they are real people, just like you, will help bring down your anxiety level.

Decision Making and Timeliness: You can make quick decisions under pressure and can make effective decisions under tight deadlines, even without all the information. You understand the importance of balancing action versus planning with respect to time lines.

In today's global environment, organizations have put a premium on the timeliness of decisions. Being first to market is seen to have higher value than getting every decision perfect as long as decisions are high quality, well thought out, and have a manageable level of risk. This scenario has forced the concept of continuous improvement to be accepted in the decision-making process.

Self-Help Tips to Improving the Decision-Making and Timeliness Skill

- Everyone would want to make perfect decisions 100 percent of the time. It's a tough concept to argue and an even tougher one to let go of! Perfectionism is really about collecting more and more information to improve your confidence level in making error-free decisions. Perfectionism is about avoiding risk and any negative reactions or consequences in being wrong. Use your intuition and make your decision when you believe you have an acceptable amount of data, and remember that making a perfect decision but being late to market does not have as much value as making a quality decision and being first.

- If you procrastinate, you will likely not make timely decisions, and the ones you do make probably will not be high quality. Start sooner, divide the task into smaller actions, and commit to completing each task in a set time interval and stick to the plan. Set a goal of completing the task and making your decision ahead of the real deadline. Begin collecting data as soon as possible so that you have the most amount of time left for analysis and decision making.

- Develop a plan with set time lines, actions, and accountabilities. Use the plan to review progress and make the review process part of your regular routine. If a time line is missed, don't just ignore it; determine what you will do to make up for the lost time and not jeopardize your deadline. As part of your plan make sure to include the target date that you establish for making your decision.

- Develop a healthy view of failure. When we fail we learn what does not work, and when we succeed we confirm what we already know. The view that needs to be developed is that failure helps lead us toward what does work, and we need to get into the habit of analyzing why something didn't work and what could be done differently to change the outcome.

- Many of us are afraid of the reaction or consequences associated with failure or making the wrong decision. Define the problem, collect your data, identify the alternatives, make your decision, develop the rationale for your decision, review your decision and rationale with leaders, and be willing to listen and modify your decision only if presented with real facts and information versus opinion and criticism.

Perspective: You understand the need to think globally and have a broad perspective on issues. You can assess the future impact of scenarios and are open-minded to see multiple views on issues and foresee potential problems or opportunities.

Each person takes his or her individual experiences, learning, and areas of interest and uses them to create connections, usually of things that were previously not known to be connected. This leads to new ideas or applications. The greater one's experiences and interests the greater the likelihood one will develop perspective as there is more to draw upon. Several years ago one of our managers was reviewing the results of a project that was initiated in his office area that involved creating a file system for how to complete each task that needed to be performed in the office area and a calendar of when the tasks needed to be performed. During the presentation he commented on how this system made cross-training easier and allowed for fewer mistakes to be made. One of the leaders in the meeting decided that he could take these principles and apply them in his production area and reduce quality problems. In doing so he created the first application of standardized work that is now being used throughout all production processes.

Self-Help Tips to Build Your Perspective Skill

- Try new things, read new books about new topics, and try new adventures.

- Become an avid reader of news and technology developments that are related to your business or industry.

- Study some historical advances, such as the development of electricity or the automobile, and look for connections that were made to bring about new advances.

- Participate in a group or project that is important and try to learn from other disciplines or functions and see how the coordination of different experiences and knowledge develops into new creative ideas.

Identify something that you've never done before, volunteer or shadow a group, and learn from the experience and attempt to make connections with things from your own background and experiences.

Presentation Skills: You are comfortable in any presentation setting and have the ability to keep the attention and control of the audience regardless of the topic. Your presentation abilities extend to include the ability to take effective control of controversial discussions and bring the group back to the objective of the presentation, and you are able to adjust during your presentation when the meeting tone or discussion is different than planned.

This competency is about having the ability to be confident and sensitive to the needs of the audience while effectively communicating your message and handling yourself on your feet. It is also about being adept at delivering a good presentation and keeping the attention of the audience. I attended a senior leadership meeting a few years ago where the marketing manager was making a presentation to the group on how we were going to change our pricing structure in Canada based on the continuous changing of the value of the Canadian dollar. Apparently the manager decided to use a presentation that had been used during the development stage with the finance team, and the presentation went deep into details that were not appropriate for this audience. As he continued to flip through his slides and tried to summarize the key points, members of the leadership team continually interrupted his presentation to ask clarifying questions as they felt obligated to try to understand the details that were put in front of them. Unfortunately, time ran out for this meeting before he could get his proposal approved, and another meeting had to be convened to present the proposal properly.

Self-Help Tips to Improve Your Presentation Skills

- Be prepared. Know your material and plan your presentation around the most important things that you want the audience to remember (a maximum of five or six key things).

- Prepare your speech or the key points you want to make sure you cover.

- Know in advance how much time you have for making the presentation and plan accordingly. Don't forget to leave time to answer questions.

- Open your presentation with a way of getting the audience's attention, perhaps a story or a summary of a critical problem that has been the subject of discussions for several members of the audience.

- Early in your presentation tell the audience what you expect at the end—their approval, a decision, information only, or some other need you may have.

- Prepare your presentation based on the audience receiving it. High-level managers will not want the same level of detail as lower-level managers, and they will be more concerned with the impact to the overall business than just the impact on a department or segment of the business.

- Practice your delivery of the presentation until you feel confident and comfortable with the material. Anticipate questions you might get and prepare in advance how you intend to respond. If possible, rehearse in the setting that you will be using for the presentation. Additionally, ask a trusted member of the group you will be presenting to if he or she would sit through a dry rehearsal and provide you with any feedback or suggestions relevant to the audience.

- Look professional. In order to be taken seriously and to be viewed as confident and the subject-matter expert you need to look the part. Everyone will be watching you, and you get to control the impression that you make on the audience. Pay attention to how you look, dress, and carry yourself, how organized you are, how prepared you are, and even how well you handle any special equipment you may be using, such as audio-visual equipment.

- If in the course of your career you expect that you will be called upon to make many presentations it may be a good idea to take a public speaking course to develop this skill professionally.

Setting Priorities: You have the ability to adjust your personal agenda to focus on what is most important. If you are confronted with several important competing tasks, you can quickly and easily identify the critical few tasks and the critical path that is most important to accomplish the major goals. You can also help others focus on the priorities and remove roadblocks.

In every sector of the economy people in careers all say, "So little time and so much to do!" There is always more to do than there are resources available to do them. No one can do it all, and you have to prioritize where you will use your time, effort, and resources. And the higher up the management hierarchy one goes, the less time is available to you.

Self-Help Tips to Increase Your Skill Level in Setting Priorities

- If you are struggling to decide which project or task will get priority it sometimes helps to look at the pros and cons of each project. What are the benefits to the business in the short term? In the long term? Are there differences in costs or resources needed? Is timing of either project a factor to consider? Is there a difference in the length of time needed to complete the project, and will the resources continue to be available for the duration? Which project will have a greater impact in meeting the goals of the business?

- In order to maximize your time and resources you need to have a well-developed plan of what you want to accomplish. Your plan should include only those activities or projects that are critical to the progress of the business. When confronted with choosing where you will spend your time, effort, or resources, always choose those things that are in your plan that are critical to the business and have the greatest impact.

- Most people tend to be influenced by what they like versus what they don't like. When making choices about where you are going to spend your time or resources it is important that you are not biased in making your selection. When possible use your plan or use data to make your decision. I had a manager who worked for me who thoroughly enjoyed spending time working directly with his customers face to face but hated doing paperwork. We learned that our department was going to be audited for compliance to our policy standards, and I asked all my managers to review their processes to ensure we would be compliant when audited. For the next several evenings I noted that one of my managers was staying at work exceptionally late. On the third evening I approached him and learned that he had been avoiding performing a number of his administrative tasks in favour of spending his time with the customer. During the audit a number of audit comments were received related to his area of responsibility as he was unable to appropriately address all the administrative issues that had been unattended to. This situation not only reflected negatively on him but as head of the department also reflected negatively on me.

- Be sensitive to the time you use of others, especially those in higher-level positions. As we said earlier, there is never enough time, and the higher you go the less time you have. Look for ways to be efficient in using other people's time. Consider preparing executive summaries; send documents or reports to people in advance of meetings so they can be prepared when you meet with them. When looking for approval of a decision prepare a pro-and-con analysis of all alternatives considered and a summary of why you selected the recommended decision.

Promotional Indicators

Individuals in a manager's role who have career aspirations to move into an executive role need to be aware that there are five competencies that are thought to be strong indicators for promotional consideration. To even be considered for an executive-level position it is critical that as a manager you demonstrate your ability especially in the following competencies.

Customer Focused: You seek to understand your customers' needs by actively interacting with them and building relationships and trust with each customer. You demonstrate care and concern for each and every customer and use the knowledge gained through customer interactions to influence product improvements and service delivery. Years ago I was assigned to a new plant as head of HR and quickly learned that HR was not a respected function at that plant. I have always believed that HR is a key enabler for any operation and as such should be totally integrated into all aspect of running the business. I decided that I would meet with each staff head and ask one simple question: "What do you need from HR that you are not getting today?" After gathering all this feedback, I met with my team and we sifted through the feedback and asked ourselves what we could do differently with our current resources to meet the needs of our customer. This initiative became the foundation for putting a customer-focused structure in place that worked and remains in use today.

I believe that every business has come to learn that without customers you have no business. History has shown that those companies that do the best job of understanding their customers, meeting their needs but surpassing their expectations and anticipating future needs before anyone else and delivering the right product or service at the right time at the right price, will win.

Self-Help Tips to Become More Customer Focused

- Look for ways to follow up and stay in touch with customers. Try to learn how satisfied they are with the product or service and whether it met their need. Also try to learn how the customer felt during the buying experience and learn to listen. Using phone follow-up surveys or written surveys can be effective tools in gathering feedback, but my experience tells me that there is no substitute for face-to-face discussion. These discussions allow for asking follow-up questions, but they also demonstrate that you are truly interested in their feedback by taking your personal time to do this.

- Every business experiences customer complaints. You need to take them seriously and be attentive to what you are being told. Where it is reasonable and it makes sense to your business, respond and react appropriately. Try to put yourself in the customer's place and ask yourself what you would expect given the same circumstances. We have learned through experience that every customer complaint deserves a response even if you feel the complaint is unjustified or even ridiculous.

- Before you introduce products or services, ask potential customers to try them and get as much feedback as possible about the product, its perceived quality, its value to the customer, what needs it meets, and anything else that can help you either improve the product or service or market it to potential customers. One dilemma that is created here that you need to be aware of is the potential of trying to be all things to all people. You will never design a product or service that will meet the needs and wants of 100 percent of the customer base. It is important that as you gather input you pay particular attention to feedback from those individuals in your target area.

- When considering introducing your product or service look at other businesses that you believe have great customer focus and try to learn why customers are satisfied and what that company does to achieve that outcome. We have also learned that it is never good enough to provide a product or service that is "as good as" your competition. Customers tend to be loyal to the products and services that they use as long as they are satisfied with them. To get customers to change their choice of product or service providers, you need to offer them something that is important to them that the current provider doesn't.

Results Oriented: You are someone who consistently meets or exceeds goals by stretching your own performance as well as the performance of others. You are always aware of the bottom line when considering alternatives and have been considered a top performer in your area. You are just as concerned with the results people around you achieve as you are your own results and are someone who makes an effort to encourage others to stretch their own goals to achieve improved results.

This skill works in combination with two other competencies: managing work and dealing with direct reports. The combination of these competencies deal with the skill of holding people accountable.

Over the years I have learned that no company can succeed in the long term by just continuing to do what they are doing today. The competition isn't standing still, and if your company does you will be bypassed. Managers and leaders have a responsibility to create an environment whereby everyone is encouraged to provide ideas and innovations that make their company or products or services better than they were yesterday. Organizations that do not create the environment where employees choose to provide their ideas are doomed to have only the few in leadership trying to come up with not only the ideas for progress and improvement but also with the burden of convincing the employees to accept and adapt to the changes. Organizations that excel at creating engaging, inclusive work environments will benefit from having everyone working to try to improve the products and services and the relationship with customers.

Intellectual Capability: You are able to deal with complex issues. Not only can you make sense of and understand concepts, but you're also able to apply the principles to other situations and effectively decipher complex issues and assist nontechnical people with understanding. People rely on you for your input and opinion on various complex issues or problems they're dealing with, because they know you can help solve the problem at hand.

Generally, intelligence is believed to be set at birth; however, science experts have routinely told us that humans use less than 10 percent of the capacity of their brain. The most common notion is that intelligence must be used on a regular basis and in doing so it is possible to make small incremental increases in one's level of intelligence. The distinction between intelligence and intellectual capability is that individuals may be intelligent but may not have the capability or experience to apply that knowledge to other situations or to be able to extract the concepts and simplify them for others to understand.

Self-Help Tips to Maximize Your Intellectual Capability

- When using your intelligence to do things such as problem solve, plan, make decisions, etc., try to remain calm and emotionless to increase the effectiveness of your brain function. If you tend to get emotional, stop what you are doing and regain your composure before reapplying yourself to the situation.

- Take time to think things through and assess what questions remain unanswered before you finalize your response or propose your solution to a problem.

- Use job aids to help you remember important steps or content. Use checklists, create pros-and-cons lists, create diagrams or flowcharts, and try different presentation alternatives, looking for ones that help you organize your thought process or methodology into logical flows.

- Consciously separate facts from opinion. When using facts it is helpful to identify the source of your information to increase the credibility of your document, presentation, or statement.

- When presenting information, if you are faced with questions do not feel compelled to respond immediately. Ask for clarification if necessary to ensure that you understand the essence of the question and only respond when you feel confident in doing so. Give yourself permission to tell people that you will think about it or research it and get back to them.

- Stay current with changes and learning applicable to your field and get involved with groups working to make advances within the field.

- Look for ways to continually challenge your mind and keep it in shape. Do puzzles; read; try to learn new things; take courses; attend workshops; and engage in dialogue with individuals you consider highly intellectual.

Workgroup Relationships: You are recognized as a team player because you can work with others to find solutions. You are cooperative, trusting, and supportive of others and can effectively solve problems through collaboration with a team.

In any business there is always some level of competitiveness between groups, departments, functions, or any other boundary that separates the type of work being performed. Because of this natural phenomenon, there are often turf issues or resistance to use something that was developed from another group. Dealing with these cross-boundary relationships will assist the business in better utilizing its resources and more efficiently using its time. The real issue here is that internally all groups should work together and see their external competitors as the threat.

In one of my past experiences I worked with a leader who was very intelligent and capable, but he was also very competitive. This leader was very capable of helping his team solve problems and increase production but was mainly interested in being recognized for his accomplishments. This leader had responsibility for machining and supplying components for an assembly operation. At this time there was a demand for more final assemblies, and as a result this leader was also required to increase the number of components supplied to the assembly line. In short order this leader was able to increase the production of components before the assembly line made the changes necessary to build more products. Instead of having his team work with the assembly line team to have the whole system capable of increasing its final output, he decided to make more components than could be used by the assembly line, hoping he would be recognized for his early accomplishments. When the assembly operation made the necessary changes, they quickly learned that the components they received from this machining line did not meet specs, and all the excess inventory that had been generated had to be scrapped—a major expense for the plant operation.

Self-Help Tips to Improve Your Workgroup Relationships

- Peers in different work groups don't have power over each other. This makes influencing, seeking understanding, building relationships, and negotiating the skills of choice. When dealing with people in other groups, look for common ground where you can help each other. Spend time asking and listening to how they see the issue that you are interested in dealing with. Build personal relationships with key individuals; get to know them personally—their interests, their family situation, their hobbies—and find things in common. When dealing across workgroups, be prepared to negotiate to get what you need done.

- Whenever you are in the presence of other workgroups, try to leave a positive impression. Don't appear aloof or impersonal; treat them the way you want to be treated.

- Be aware that regardless of the individuals there may be some natural biases or internal politics working against you in your efforts to build relationships across workgroups. Try to understand what is at the root of them and work to dispel them, mostly by setting the example with your own behaviour.

- Individuals may perceive you as political or even highly competitive in your efforts to build relationships. Generally this is a function of not having built trust, and the early stages of building relationships may appear to be self-serving. When dealing with issues across workgroups, especially when the individuals involved have not developed a working relationship, start by sharing your thinking and logic on issues and ask others to share theirs; focus on the end goal and not how to get there—leave that to allow for a flexible solution.

- Don't forget to say thank you and to use positive reinforcement when someone helps you with a situation. You may even consider informing the individual's supervisor about what the person did, how it helped you and the business, and how much you appreciated the assistance. Take time to celebrate the wins and include individuals from other workgroups that assisted in the accomplishment.

- If in your efforts to work across groups you find that an individual is uncooperative or doesn't play fair, confront the individual directly and give him or her the opportunity to explain, save face, or correct the situation. Remember that the most important thing here is getting the task accomplished.

Quality Decisions: You consistently make good decisions through analysis of the situation and through considering your own experiences and knowledge. People know you can be relied upon to make good-quality decisions and will seek you out for advice or involvement when they're facing problems they don't know how to solve.

I was fortunate in my career that I had individuals whom I had built relationships with over time that I could rely upon to discuss issues with as well as possible problem-solving approaches. As such I always made myself available to help others. I always learned and also taught others that decisions must be based on data and not on opinions. I also learned that decisions need to be made from a variety of alternatives and the decision made needs to be based on the circumstances at that time, not just on what decision was made previously.

Good decisions flow from good data, proper analysis, wisdom, experience, and judgment. Making quality decisions requires the patience to collect the data and being open and confident enough to involve others and ask for their opinions and ideas and then having the ability to make the final call. Everyone makes mistakes and bad decisions. The challenge is to consistently increase the percentage of time that the right decisions are made and to know when you just cannot afford to make a wrong one and then avoiding it.

There is always pressure for decisions to be made quickly. Unless the situation is dire, you need to resist the pressure and ensure that at least some data is collected so that a few possible alternatives can be identified and an informed decision can be made. Making a poor-quality decision may not be the end of the world. No one will remember that you were under pressure to make the decision you made, but they will remember that you made it!

Self-Help Tips to Increase the Likelihood of Making Quality Decisions

- We all have biases, prejudices, and opinions. The challenge is not to let them get in the way of making solid-quality decisions. Before you make any final decision it is important to ask yourself if any of your biases have come into play in making your decision.

- Check to ensure that your decision is based on data and facts and not on assumptions or opinions.

- As we discussed in the problem-solving competency, make sure you have a well-defined problem definition and have asked "why" enough times to feel confident that you are in fact dealing with the root cause.

- Have you collected data in the right way? Are you comfortable that the data is reflective of the actual situation? Analyse the data to identify trends and patterns and then identify alternatives for resolving the problem. Involve others and confirm that they identify the problem the same way you do. Get their advice and opinion regarding which alternative has the greatest likelihood of success.

- Once you have completed your analysis and considered the alternatives and you are satisfied that there are no other questions needing to be answered, then either make your decision or choose to sleep on it (to give your brain a chance to rethink everything one last time) and make your decision in the morning.

- If you are required to make complex decisions on a regular basis you may want to study or learn to use a decision-making model to assist you in understanding what questions to ask, what principles to follow, and the rigor associated with using a common process. Commonly used decision-making models include the Pugh's method and decision matrix or the Bayesian Team Support method (also commonly called the Accord method).

Setting the Stage for an Executive Role

There are also a number of competencies that are required for effective performance in an executive role. You need to be aware of these additional competencies and look for opportunities to develop them or demonstrate that you have them if you are serious about pursuing a role as an executive. For individuals with potential, these competencies are believed to be developed at this stage of one's career and should be demonstrated as often as possible under the right circumstances. The competencies that are necessary for an executive's role include the following.

Dealing with Uncertainty: You manage uncertainty well and are not afraid of change. You are even tempered when priorities shift or decisions are forthcoming and can quickly move on to new tasks and change your focus when the current task is at a standstill. You have a strong tolerance for risk.

Most people have no difficulty performing tasks or making the right decision when they are clearly presented with all the right information and given detailed instructions or direction. Unfortunately, that situation does not always exist, and individuals with this skill are able to make good decisions with limited information and direction or solve problems that have never been solved before.

In my past experiences at collective bargaining I have had many situations where uncertainty was the situation of the day. Patience is crucial when dealing with uncertainty, and you have to be prepared to focus on the end point, not how you get there. In planning for collective bargaining, a lot of preparation goes into identifying solutions to problems as you would define them. It is not until you are actually in the process that the real definition of the problem is identified, thus opening up a range of possible alternatives to explore. The key here is being willing to deal with changing circumstances and changing priorities.

Self-Help Tips to Feel More Comfortable in Dealing with Uncertainty

- The essence of dealing with uncertainty is becoming comfortable with the notion that you will make mistakes and generally have to take some heat as a result. Individuals who are most adept at dealing in this situation have learned to break the situation or problem into smaller increments and then try different alternatives that give them immediate feedback. Then they progress with this incremental amount of information. This allows them to course-correct along the way and enhances the likelihood that they will ultimately make good decisions or at least better decisions based on the situation; after all, for the most part they are somewhat shooting in the dark.

- Most people are most comfortable when they are in control and have knowledge about everything around them. Some people enjoy taking on the challenge of being the first to solve a problem or finding a new solution to an old problem. Developing your skill in dealing with uncertainty requires one to be comfortable dealing with the unknown, experimenting, breaking new ground, or learning new things. Become adventurous—try new places, experience new things, and don't do advance research but just go ahead and learn from the experience.

- Dealing with uncertainty starts by getting the best definition possible for the problem and then trying to figure out what caused it. Here again, defining the problem starts by asking "why" several times to ensure that the root cause of the problem is identified. This will force you to not begin by trying to solve an ill-defined problem.

- When confronted with a complex problem that is difficult to understand, try to make the problem visual. Use a diagram or flowchart to show the elements contributing to the problem, the process flow, and how each element affects the outcome. This will help you identify what is working and what isn't.

- One of the biggest inhibitors for individuals in developing this competency is stress. We get stressed when we are dealing with ambiguity—it takes us out of our comfort zone. We are not at our best when we feel anxious or frustrated, because we don't want to make mistakes. When you are in this situation and are feeling stressed, stop what you are doing and go and work on something else that allows you to feel safe and in control. When you gather your composure and feel more confident, go back and work on the problem again. You will likely find that subconsciously your brain was continuing to work on the issue while you were doing the other task and you are now more likely to make progress.

Negotiation Skill: Your negotiation skills quickly gain trust from others, and you have the ability to be both direct and forceful or caring and sympathetic depending on the situation. You can put yourself in another person's shoes while looking for win-win solutions to issues. While you are a strong negotiator and will go for what is necessary, you understand that the relationship needs to be preserved beyond the negotiation process.

The essence of negotiation is the process of finding common ground among two or more parties at the lowest cost with both sides leaving the situation feeling good about the experience. In any negotiation it is highly unlikely that one party gets exactly what they wanted and the other side leaves satisfied. If negotiations end in one side winning and the other losing, there is a high likelihood that the losing party will avoid negotiating with the other side in the future or the losing party may not actively support what was agreed to following negotiations.

Self-Help Tips to Increase Your Skill in Negotiating

- In advance of negotiating look for ways to build relationships with key individuals. Try to understand their values, how they think, and how they generally do business.

- In advance of negotiating, make sure the other party is aware of issues that are important to you (or the business) and why they are important.

- In negotiations put the issue on the table but don't get locked into one solution. To resolve an important issue it needs to be looked at from both perspectives, and the real end game is finding a solution that deals with the issue and both sides can live with.

- Negotiation is most effective when the number of people involved is small—the fewer the better. Look for opportunities to have sidebar discussions so that individuals can talk openly and freely about their issues, what their sticking points are, and what might satisfy their interests.

- Always remember that generally the individuals involved in the negotiations will likely have to present the agreement to others with a vested interest in the outcome, so each side has to be aware of the need to help equip the other side with the logic and rationale to sell the agreement to their constituents.

- Listen, listen, listen. In any negotiations it is critical to look for signs that will indicate what is most important to resolve for the other side. Without knowing what is important to the other side, you will not likely be able to reach a reasonable agreement.

- It is common for emotions to be high in any negotiations. Avoid emotional responses. Deal with facts and issues only. Ask clarifying questions to be able to best define the issue at hand. If emotions run too high and too long, look for an opportunity to delay, take issues off line, or meet separately in a smaller group of key individuals with the greatest knowledge of the issue.

- Always know your bottom line in any negotiation and be prepared to walk away if necessary.

Strategic Thinker: You're always anticipating future trends and making plans accordingly. You are someone who looks to create competitive strategies to stay ahead of the competition and can see future consequences of actions or inactions. Not only are you able to think strategically, but you can articulate visions and possibilities based on that thinking, and you have a broad perspective and knowledge.

This is one of the competencies that are in short supply in the general population, and it is also one of the most difficult to develop. Most businesses are very good at doing what they do today, but this skill is about seeing what needs to be done to be ready for tomorrow and to stay ahead of the competition. This competency becomes more and more critical the higher up one goes in the organization. The ability to see the signs and the trends and predict where the market is headed or anticipate a shift in consumer preference or a downturn in the economy impacting your business are critically important to the long-term survival of the business. Strategy is about looking at all the variables and interactions and predicting the most likely outcome. It involves uncertainty, assumptions, and a general understanding of systems and how different things work together or interact with each other.

A key executive whom I worked with was very gifted in this competency. He was able to predict that with technology changing at a rapid pace with home computers, cell phones, and entertainment devices the auto industry needed to rethink how cars were designed to get ahead of the competition in this area. This lead to the development of the OnStar system that is now installed on all GM vehicles.

Self-Help Tips to Improve Your Strategic Thinking Ability

- If you believe you have this skill but you are not recognized as having it, you may need to learn to speak strategically. Basically this means that you take the time to analyse trends, look at possibilities, and explore customer needs and then discuss these on a regular basis with leaders in the organization. It also means that you have thought about the future and the consequences of not being prepared for future trends. Like most other disciplines, strategic thinkers have their own buzz words or code that indicates they have strategic ability (words like strategic intent or core capabilities or co-evolution). Read books and articles from *Harvard Business Review* or *Leadership and Strategy* to learn the code.

- Strategic plans provide a roadmap to leaders to help guide the future direction of the business. Most strategic plans don't actually materialize as outlined, but they do serve the purpose of bringing focus to the choices leaders need to make to move the business forward. These plans provide direction for the organization and also signal what is important to senior leadership. Generally organizations develop strategic plans as a way of moving the organization forward, and they also set measurable targets and time lines for progress to be made. These plans serve as a reference point for executives in the organization to develop objectives that then flow through the organization and link everyone to a set of initiatives that will help achieve the objectives set and the organization's targets.

- Being curious and asking yourself questions such as "what would happen if …" lends itself to taking people out of their day-to-day focus and allowing them to consider possibilities for tomorrow. Talk to new people. Join new organizations. Read different books. Develop new interests. All of these activities have the potential to broaden your thinking and may allow you to better see what may happen tomorrow.

- To be effective as a strategic thinker you have to be able to set aside facts and data and try to use intuition and feeling. You have to accept the fact that most strategies cannot be proven and that if you get into a debate the strategy generally cannot be supported by data. People who excel at strategy force the conversation. They push others to think outside the box, and they help others imagine the possibilities. Being a strategic thinker is not about settling for some simplified statement about what will happen tomorrow; it is about seeing what is possible and helping organizations figure out how to get there. Because we are dealing with the future there are no facts or data that will support what decisions should be made to be ready for the future. It is an imperfect science, and some leaders have a great "feel" for not only what is possible but also what will be accepted in the marketplace. A brilliant leader I knew once told me that the secret behind strategy is not to wait until you can see the future but to create it and be the first to market.

- Because this competency is so difficult to develop it is virtually in a category of "you either have it or you don't." There are a few people in the world who are considered strategy experts, and they have written books and articles on strategy that quite frankly a lot of people don't understand. If you are inclined to enhance your ability in this area you may want to consider taking strategy courses or participating in a strategy workshop or attending conferences hosted by one of the world-recognized strategy experts. If you aren't prepared to do that and you don't believe in strategy, focus on your other competencies and leave strategy up to the strategists.

- Most organizations have learned that not all businesses require a strategist on staff. What is really needed is a healthy regard for the value of strategy, a willingness to spend the time with a strategy expert, and a willingness to bring in the resource when you need it.

Political Sensitivity: You're knowledgeable and sensitive to how people and organization works. You can anticipate political problems and adjust your approach accordingly as you understand that politics cannot be avoided, so you compensate for its existence. The distinction between being politically sensitive and being political is that if you are political you are generally not trusted, whereas being sensitive you are aware that politics exist and you try to work around them as best you can.

Each organization is made up of a complex blend of egos, rivalries, and competing interests and agendas. Many of these parts tend to be silos led by someone with a large ego who tries to protect his or her entity, grow it, and even seclude it from outside influences. These are simply facts in every organization, and people who are skilled in this area are aware of these egos and influences and learn to work with it as another variable that has to be considered in getting things done.

I have worked with many executives who used politics to get to their position. I have generally found that over time these individuals find themselves on their own and are not trusted or respected and have a difficult time getting things done. Executives who got to their positions by their skills, abilities, and achievements are well respected, and people are drawn to them as mentors. These executives have made work relationships wherever they have been assigned and have created a positive work environment amongst their peers and employees.

Self-Help Tips to Increase Your Political Sensitivity

- Develop a reputation for having integrity and being trustworthy. These attributes generally will help eliminate any perception that you have your own agenda.

- Prior to approaching a particular group or individual whom you believe is political in nature, decide in advance what style, tone, and method will enhance the likelihood of getting the best result. This may involve watching what others have tried and their result or asking others what approaches have been successful in dealing with this group or individual.

- Get to know who the power players are. Who has the most influence on key decisions and resources? Attempt to build a positive relationship with these individuals by finding things in common and things that you both can agree on. Look for their assistance when they can influence key decisions affecting outcomes impacting your goals.

- Watch for nonverbal clues in meetings to determine if you are getting support or resistance (not paying attention, staring, crossing arms, frowning). If you see that the issue lacks support, try to open up the dialogue by asking a question. Try to get those that are resistant to say why and what would get them to support the idea.

- Sometimes you just need to bargain. Sometimes you need to go to individuals who are resisting giving you the support you need and tell them what you need and ask them what they need to get their support.

- Keep conflicts out of issue discussions. Focus on the nature of the problem rather than the individual presenting it. If an agreement cannot be reached, try to agree on a process that can be used to get agreement.

- Be prepared with multiple plans if you suspect a political stop. Stay focused on the end goal and remain flexible on how you get there.

To be considered for an executive role, an employee needs to be viewed as having potential beyond the current position but also demonstrate a capacity to learn or be "learning agile." Learning skills and driving for results are generally the greatest predictors of promotion at any level. Learning agile people tend to see new connections to traditional problems; they are able to effectively deal with tough situations; they can deal with the discomfort that comes with change; and they deliver results through teams and personal drive. All of these tendencies result from finding balance between being results focused, questioning conventional wisdom, focusing on people, and leading change.

It is often difficult to get into positions that will give individuals the chance to develop some competencies that are learned through practical experience. Research has shown that the number one developer of competencies is job change into a more challenging role. It is estimated that 70 percent of all development that occurs comes when the role or assignment brings with it a significant chance of failure. Research also shows that the number two developer of competencies comes from a challenging project or task where one either meets the objective or fails. It is often misunderstood that just because someone has been given a particular assignment that does not necessarily mean that certain competencies were successfully developed. Research shows that without the chance of failure, very little development will actually occur.

Chapter 5

Executive Role

An executive is an individual whom the organization relies upon to develop strategies to lead the business in achieving its objectives. In this role the executive is expected to work across functional lines with other executives and allocate resources to achieve organizational goals having the greatest impact on the overall business.

To be successful in this category an executive is generally recognized for his or her ability to understand the total business, develop strategies, deal with major changes and resistance points, sell the vision of the future state, and create an environment where everyone knows what needs to be done, has the skills and resources to do it, and wants to actively participate in the accomplishment.

In addition to the competencies referenced in the previous chapter (dealing with ambiguity, negotiations skills, strategic thinking, and political sensitivity) the following unique competencies have also been associated with performance success in an executive career category. If this describes you, there is a strong possibility you would succeed in this type of career path.

Understands the Business: You have an understanding for how a business functions, and specifically the competition and the business strategies. You make yourself aware of how trends, technology, and business practices are affecting the business and anticipate the need for change to prepare for future impacts on the business.

This competency has two legs: first it relates to understanding business in general, and second it relates to having an understanding of your specific business, how it functions, and how the pieces of the business interact as well as knowing about the total industry or business sector. Without having an understanding of the business, it is difficult to understand what the business priorities are, how they will affect the business or its competitive position, or how you can help the business meet its goals and objectives.

Self-Help Tips to Improve Your Understanding of the Business

- If you don't have an understanding of your business, take time to talk to people who do. Find out what is involved in delivering the products or services to the customer. What processes are used and why? What functions are performed, and what are the capabilities of the organization? Who is the competition, and what is the business working on to stay ahead? How does the business stack up against the competition, and what can you do to help? Volunteer to become involved in tasks that will give you a broader perspective of the business. Meet with key individuals in each function and learn what their primary duties are and why they are important to the business.

- Talk to customers of your products or services and learn how your business is viewed externally. Years ago in the auto industry it was critical to learn that customers were not satisfied with the service they were getting from the dealers despite their level of satisfaction with the products. This became a major initiative inside the company to help change the service level as well as the reputation of the dealer network.

- Take courses; read business magazines; follow business trends; learn what factors have the greatest impact on the business; join a business organization; join national organizations for your industry and attend conferences.

- Learn to analyse problems from a total business perspective. Read case studies of successful companies as well as unsuccessful ones. Learn what the key factors in each were.

Read several company prospectuses and see the areas that they highlight as important and what their main challenges and areas of concern are.

Creative: You are original and unique in your ideas and look for a connection between unrelated topics. During brainstorming sessions with others, you offer out-of-the box ideas and new perspectives on old ideas.

This skill involves looking for connections that did not previously exist (i.e., using reshaping plastics on vehicle body parts that do not affect the safety of the vehicle), searching for what others have done in other businesses or industries (i.e., applying coatings on paint to reduce the effect of UV rays on paint colour), and brainstorming with others (preferably individuals from a variety of disciplines). There are many systemic barriers that reduce the likelihood of creativity, such as being told to restrain ourselves, being focused on what we are good at, being afraid to look foolish, or being aware of just how others deal with mistakes being made. A strong leader needs to create the environment where creativity is valued and mistakes are viewed as opportunities for learning. Remove the barriers and encourage creativity and innovation.

From a business perspective, innovation starts by knowing what your customers want that they are willing to buy; knowing what features or attributes of the product or service are most important to customers and most affect their purchasing decision; and getting an understanding of why noncustomers don't buy your products. The next challenge is identifying the right ideas for new products and services that are most likely to be successful in the market and finally having the skill to take the right ideas and manage their development through to introducing the new products or services in the market.

Self-Help Tips to Build Your Creative/Innovative Skill

- Remove barriers and remember that being creative is about going outside the rules (i.e., allow employees to experiment and try out ideas without fear of negative consequences). It is about not being cautious or afraid to make mistakes. It's about sharing ideas and thoughts without trying to rationalize or defend them. Creativity involves looking at things from a variety of angles and looking in areas you wouldn't normally think to look. Remove yourself from the normal work environment (which subconsciously represents boundaries and parameters to you) and look for a place where you can have fun and be open and comfortable.

- When in a creativity session select people with different backgrounds, different disciplines, different personality types, and different experiences. This will give you the best chance of ensuring that you get many perspectives and come up with the best and most creative solution.

- Start by defining the problem you want to solve or the issue you want to deal with. Make sure you have the right definition of the problem and you are not trying to solve a symptom (ask "why" five times to get at the root of the problem). Don't accept first responses or ideas and close the discussion. Make sure everyone participates and talks out loud. Creative ideas or solutions often flow from the building upon others' ideas or thoughts. Where possible look at data and sort it in different ways so you can make sense of it and see multiple possible solutions.

- Take the time to try different things and learn from the process as well as the outcome. Experiment, do pilots, try many low-cost alternatives, and see what you learn.

- Once an idea is selected you need to manage it through its development, approval, and introduction into the marketplace. Every new idea needs a champion who will deal with the challenges of getting others to embrace introducing it into the company's portfolio. You may experience push back from those who may be negatively impacted by its introduction. Prepare yourself with full knowledge of why it makes sense to introduce the new product, how it meets a need of current customers or potential new customers, and how this product or service differs from others offered by the competition.

Visionary: You can create and effectively communicate a vision of the future that inspires people and describes a future state that people want to be part of. You can manage strategy and objectives toward the achievement of that vision. Research shows that those businesses with inspiring visions tend to do better than those that don't. The reason for having a vision is to define what you see for the business in the future for your customers, employees, shareholders, and community. It is a statement about what is possible and what you want the business to stand for.

The right vision for your business can have benefits, such as the following:

- It can motivate and energize your employees.

- It can give employees a greater purpose than just their personal needs, and it can help create pride.

- It can help establish a standard of excellence in the business.

- It can focus the business on continuous improvement versus maintaining the status quo.

- It can guide leaders in decision making and setting direction and priorities for the business.

- It can help define what the priorities of the business should be and where resources, investments, and energy should be focused.

Self-Help Tips to Improve Your Visionary Skill

- Creating an effective vision statement that inspires is a difficult task. Because a vision or mission statement is not created on a regular basis, many leaders choose to bring in an expert to assist them in creating their statements. Probably the best example of a vision statement is from General Electric: "We bring good things to life." I am sure you have heard this before. It has remained the same and guided the leadership at GE through their down periods and through their restructuring. It has also been a staple in their advertising.

Characteristics of an Effective Vision:

- The vision must be realistic (it must be within the realm of possibility for your business from where you are now).

- The vision must be credible (it must be believable, especially to employees and people within the business).

- The vision must be attractive (it must inspire employees and motivate them to want to be part of the future that is envisioned for the business).

- The vision must be in the future (it must be an achievable point in time, say in three to ten years).

- The vision must be well articulated and easily understood.

- Once a vision statement is created it needs to have life breathed into it. Employees generally will not follow the words on paper unless the actions of the leadership are aligned to the vision. If the behaviours that are expected in the vision statement are different from what employees have been experiencing to date, don't be surprised if you do not see a change in the behaviour of employees right away. Employees will wait to see if the vision is real and whether leadership is really committed to the vision not with words but with their actions and the decisions that they make. Once the employees are convinced that the change is real, then a change in employee behaviour can be expected.

To be considered for an executive role an employee needs to be viewed as fully developed in the above competencies, and in particular be highly proficient at understanding the business, be in command and control, and be extremely organized. It should be noted that in this category many of the competencies are ones that are not generally found in the general population or are difficult to develop. Accordingly, most organizations have a very small list of employees who demonstrate potential to become an executive in their business. Even more critical is the understanding that in most companies, employees under consideration for future executive positions generally have assignments in both the individual role category and the people manager category prior to be considered for an executive position.

As stated previously, individuals must embrace each assignment in each category and be focused on being the best they can be based on their skill set and interests. Individuals need to take the initiative to develop the competencies that are related to success for an executive role *while at the same time trying to be the best they can be in their current role.* The best approach is to develop the competencies for the executive category and then look for opportunities to show that you possess these competencies when opportunities present themselves.

Chapter 6

Sixteen Ways to End Your Career

Regardless of your skill set, your proficiency with key success competencies, or any other characteristic that sets you apart from others, you need to keep in mind that there are also traits or actions that could put an end to your career.

Just as you have to manage your career over a long period of time, growing your positive characteristics and skills to advance, you also need to avoid the situations that will end your career and virtually erase all of your progress. Unfortunately, once you have experienced a career-ending event or have shown a particular characteristic, it becomes almost impossible to overcome.

Here are sixteen ways to end your career. If your goal is to succeed, you'll need to avoid them!

1) Inability to Adapt to Differences

It's not possible to reach success in your career if you're inflexible and unable to adapt to changes and differences. If you have trouble working with and adapting to new or different bosses, strategies, coworkers, or specific assignments, you can kiss your career good-bye. These are characteristics of employees who have "jobs," not leaders or successful professionals with careers. People who are unable to adapt to differences and accept change might disagree inappropriately or too vocally with top management and would have a very difficult time working with a person they disagreed with.

Recently I had a very talented young professional who was identified as having the right set of competencies for executive potential. As we planned his career path, his assignment required a transfer to another geographic location within the company. Early in his new assignment the leader of this area came to discuss her observations of this individual. She told me that this individual was having great difficulty accepting that he was in another environment and that despite coaching efforts his behaviour continued. She described the situation as whenever he had business dealings both with his staff and his peers he continuously told them, "When I was in my former assignment that's not the way we did it." In short order he had managed to frustrate everyone with his inability to accept change and adapt to his new environment to the point where it became necessary to move him to another assignment.

Another individual had worked with a leader for over ten years in three different assignments. The leader retired, and a new leader from another part of the company was assigned into that position. It was very apparent that the leadership styles of the two individuals were very different. The former leader gave this individual the direction he needed but then got out of the way and let the individual plan and execute on his own. The new leader had a need to know what work was being done in his new area, and he required all his direct reports to have a weekly update meeting to discuss progress, identify roadblocks, and review plans to meet objectives and time lines of their projects. This individual felt that he didn't need to attend these reviews as he had already demonstrated his ability to execute with his previous leader. After several discussions with the new manager the individual asked for a transfer to a different part of the company. This employee's refusal to conform to the new requirement from his leader was quickly noted and shared with all other leaders in the company, thus damaging his reputation.

2) Lack of Attention to Detail

Not everyone has a mind for the details. If you're unable to deliver on all details of commitments or regularly miss deadlines after scrambling around trying to meet deadlines at the last minute, you're setting yourself up for an abrupt end to your career. People who claim to "work well under pressure" often overlook the basic requirements that need to be performed and miss important details that make all the difference between a job well done and one that's barely done, or perhaps not done at all.

3) Excessive Focus on Career

Having goals and being focused is a good thing, so how is having excessive focus on your career a way to put an end to that career? People who are excessively focused on their career will make decisions based on the impact those decisions have on their career. This means they're willing to sacrifice others if it will make them look good. People who excessively focus on advancing their career at all costs will do things that they feel makes them look good in the eyes of leaders instead of focusing on things that result in the greater good for peers and subordinates. If you have excessive focus on your career, chances are you're willing to use politics to advance, and this is often the path to career demise.

4) Extreme Egotism

In any business environment, people who are interested in advancing their career will generally have a high level of self-confidence and a healthy ego, but both are tempered by a respect for others. If you ignore the input and ideas of others and believe that you are always right or have the right answers, you're going to cause the people you work with to feel undervalued and inferior. People who are overly egotistical do not work well in teams and will be unable to advance their careers successfully.

5) Lack of Dependability

If it becomes obvious to your coworkers and managers that you can't be relied upon and that you regularly don't do what you say you will do, you can forget about building a successful career. Not being dependable also includes moving on to other tasks before you finish previous tasks or being unable to keep confidences in the workplace.

6) Unwillingness to Learn

One method of ending your career is being unwilling to learn. Avoiding training and learning opportunities like workshops or reading and using the same tactics over and over again despite the potential for new and better ways to do things is not going to win you any steps on the career ladder. People who are unwilling to learn generally do not look for input from other people when faced with new challenges and may even feel like they know everything they need to know. This belief will not lend itself well to advancing in your career.

7) Lack of Self-Control

Another good way to sabotage your career is to lack self-control. If stress causes you to act unpredictably or you make irrational decisions when you're under pressure, you'll be passed over for promotions. You can't openly show negative emotions and become sarcastic or aggressive when you're stressed and expect to take on leadership roles in an organization. The higher you move up in your career within an organization, the more responsibility you'll probably have and the more stress and pressure you will experience. At higher levels it becomes increasingly important to manage emotions, because you will be observed by others and employees tend to replicate the actions and behaviours of leaders (the belief being that these behaviours are valued by leadership and helped get this person to that level in the organization).

8) Overly Defensive Behaviour

If you're the type of person who rationalizes your errors or failures and is not open to constructive feedback, you'll quickly end your career. Having poor listening skills or openly blaming others when thing go wrong or being closed minded on personal development with the attitude that you have no reason to improve will not help you advance in your career.

9) Failure to Use Teams Effectively

Here's another great way to end your career: avoid the use of teams and the value that comes from team involvement. Or decide to use teams but don't share the purpose or goals of the team work with the members of the team and make individual assignments instead of trying to benefit from team input. You can end your career by ignoring the need for team development and camaraderie.

10) Ineffective Staffing Choices

Part of growing a successful career requires that you're able to select effective staff with complementary skills. A good way to end your career is to select people who are just like you instead of choosing people with a wide range of skill sets. If you're a poor judge of people and what they're capable of, you won't succeed.

11) Lack of Sensitivity

If you are not concerned with the needs and feelings of others and do not relate well to others, you may as well look for a job instead of a career. You can't advance through the ranks of a corporation with a cold or intimidating style, being unapproachable, or avoiding others except when you need them. This is a surefire way to squash a potential career. (Note: I am aware that some organizations actually embrace an intimidating style believing that this type of leadership will keep employees "in line" and help them get the results they desire. In the short term, this type of leader might get some results, but ultimately these same companies come to realize that this style actually "freezes an organization," preventing employees from engaging or giving their discretionary effort and simply doing what they are told to do. They also learn that when employees work under this type of executive they provide the least amount of effort that keeps them out of trouble because no one wants to be noticed for fear of negative attention.)

12) Lack of Focus on Direction or Strategy

You can end your career by failing to see the future impact of your decisions or if you are consumed by details and "doing" to the point that you forget to set direction and think through some advanced planning.

13) Single-Advocate Dependence

If you have learned everything you know from one person within the organization to the point of being dependent on that person, your career will stop if your advocate leaves the organization or is reassigned to an area where he or she can no longer represent your interests.

14) Overuse of a Dominant Skill

It's great to have strengths you can rely on to make things happen, but if you have one dominant skill that you overuse, you may be in danger of thinking you don't need to develop other skills. If this describes you, then there's a good chance you're about to end your career.

15) Lack of Delegation Skills

Career advancement requires delegation skills. If you don't empower others and insist on doing most of the work yourself, you're not going to make a good leader. If you do delegate but constantly interfere and check on the progress or make corrections rather than develop and teach others, you won't get much effort out of your team. I had a manager working for me who was exceptional in his ability to problem-solve, analyse situations, and generally get things done. When business was running normally he would effectively use his staff and support them when needed, but he always wanted to know what they were working on and the progress they were making. In this area we had many crisis situations to deal with, and when he was called upon to get his team to deal with these crisis situations he was unable to delegate as he felt that no one could handle the situation as effectively or in as timely a manner as he could. The result of this was that whenever there was a crisis this manager would work all hours of the night and weekends and his staff would sit back and watch.

16) Failure to Get Results

Finally, if you are someone who fails to get results, you may as well wave good-bye to a successful career. Whether you're unable to get results from others, unable to meet goals and objectives, or can't hold yourself or others accountable, the end result is the same: no result!

I have found that one of the best ways to avoid any of these traits from ruining your career is to actively ask for feedback not only from your supervisor but also from your peers, employees, and customers of your service, *and* you have to be prepared to react to the feedback. If a trait is identified that you need to deal with, don't hesitate to look for mentors or approach people who excel at that trait and ask if they would coach you in that area. If you ask for feedback, people will feel more comfortable giving you honest feedback because you will be perceived as "ready" to receive it. If you wait until someone provides it, you may learn that it may never come or it may come too late, after the damage is done.

Chapter 7

Being on Your Best Behaviour

We have spent a lot of time getting to know the main competency differentiators between individual contributors, managers, and executives. Now I want to focus on what I call the "behaviour basics."

In spite of having the right skills and abilities, there are some very telling behavioural traits that will allow you to get noticed, which is the "foot in the door" to any advancement opportunity. I want to dedicate this chapter to helping you understand the behavioural basics. If you don't demonstrate these basics you may never get the opportunity to use your talents, even if you are highly skilled at all the right competencies and have the potential.

The following are considered "best behaviours" for being successful in the workplace and for being selected for advancement opportunities: So let's start at the beginning.

Best Behaviour #1: Your Appearance Counts

In spite of what the actual dress code or policies are for your company, the way you dress, your appearance, cleanliness, and neatness, creates a first impression about your professionalism. At some point, leadership will be asking themselves whether they want a person who dresses like (fill in the blank for someone dressing overly casual or sloppy) to represent the company to external clients or be a role model for other employees.

As you already know "you never get a second chance to make a first impression."

Appearance counts all the time—from the job application to the interview to meetings and appointments, right through to every day on the job. Don't forget that you represent your company, and your image is that company's essence. Your employer's goal is to have employees project a favourable image; your goal is to represent the employer and yourself in a favourable way. Your first impression may influence how people react to the way you look and present yourself in the beginning, even if you look and act differently later on. The way you look and act at work is critical to your success on the job.

Why do some people dress in conservative suits to go to work? The answer is that you appear more competent and professional and you portray confidence clad in this attire as opposed to just casual dress. Dressing for success gets you noticed and recognized and enables you to have influence. So take the time to make a good impression on others. Having a good appearance also makes you feel great about yourself, helping improve your self-confidence and your attitude.

Business Attire: The clothing you choose to wear to work will depend on what everyone else is wearing and the industry you work in. Look around at what your coworkers and managers are wearing to get a feel for the type of clothing that is acceptable, and then choose well-fitting, clean, ironed, or pressed clothing. Be careful of being too flashy with your clothing choices so that you are taken seriously on the job, but keep a professional appearance.

Personal Grooming: Just as important as the clothing you choose to wear is your personal grooming habits. Your hair should always be clean and neatly styled. If it's currently all over the place, have a stylist cut it so that it is easily maintained for the professional environment. Brush your teeth before work every morning, and if you tend to have breath issues, keep breath mints or a toothbrush and toothpaste at work to use as needed. You should manage body odours appropriately so that you always smell fresh and pleasant, but beware of cologne or perfume. Wearing a little cologne or perfume is okay (if company policies don't prohibit their use), provided you put it on well in advance of arriving at work and only use a tiny amount so that it is subtle and not overpowering. Keep your eyeglasses clean. Men should always be clean shaven, and women who wear makeup should apply it so that it looks natural rather than painted on.

Caring for Company Belongings: If you receive company equipment, such as cars, phones, voice recorders, computers, or any other electronics, treat it as a privilege. How you care for these items is as important to making a good impression at work as your personal appearance is. Keeping company belongings clean, organized, and properly cared for will create the idea that you are efficient and trustworthy.

Best Behaviour #2: Be Trustworthy

Trust is when people around you have accepted that you are capable and committed to doing what you are expected to do. If you have a reputation for being honest and reliable in the workplace, then you will be considered trustworthy. When people trust you, they are more inclined to like you, and it makes a huge difference in how people will treat you.

When someone is not trustworthy, people tend to steer clear of them whenever possible. A person who is trusted receives more opportunities than those who are not considered trustworthy. Keep in mind that failure to deliver something you've committed to or promised will be perceived as a betrayal. Fail to deliver enough times and you'll be considered untrustworthy.

Trust in the Workplace: There is a link between the successes of an organization and the amount of trust among employees. When people see their coworkers and the management as trustworthy, there is a higher level of commitment and performance levels and less need for close monitoring or management controls over employee output.

Trust and Competitive Advantage: In the business world, the level of trust among workplace relationships is directly related to the amount of sales and profits a company earns and the employee turnover. The management's ability to earn trust from its employees is likely to give the company an advantage over its competitors.

Best Behaviour #3: Build Relationships

Have you ever noticed that successful people have long-term relationships with friends and coworkers? That they tend to make friends easily and get along with just about everyone they meet? The ability to build relationships is necessary to successful career advancement.

Building relationships starts with building trust. There can never be a strong or long-term relationship among people who do not trust one another. Think about your personal relationships and the benefits that come from having strong relationships with friends, significant others, and family members. When you have a good relationship, you often have an idea what the other person is thinking or feeling without it having to be said. Relationships in the workplace help us understand why someone might react a certain way to a situation and allow us to take care of business easier because it eliminates the need to uncover the "hidden agenda."

How to Build Strong Relationships in the Workplace

- ***Have Empathy:*** Learning how to relate to another person's feelings, situation, and motives for actions is the key to building good relationships. When you can recognize the concerns other people have and really put yourself in their shoes, you can be proactive in the workplace or at least anticipate problems before they occur. Having empathy will help you connect with the people in your workplace, improve your trustworthiness, and strengthen relationships.

- ***Become a Good Listener:*** If you aren't one already, learn how to be a good listener. Listening is more than just hearing what someone is saying. Learn to "listen" to others' body languages, the tone of voice they're using, the emotions hidden in the words, and how it applies to the situation. Being a good listener strengthens relationships.

- ***Watch for Nonverbal Communication:*** Much of what people say is shared through nonverbal communication. If you learn how to recognize these signs, you'll discover what people actually think and feel may be completely different from what they're actually saying.

- ***Stop Interrupting People:*** When people are talking to you, learn to be fully present at that moment. Don't check your e-mail during a conversation, don't glance at the clock on the wall or your watch, and don't dismiss their concerns without hearing everything they have to say. Allow them to fully express their concerns or information before you give any advice or make comments. If you don't have time to discuss their issue at that moment, then schedule a more convenient time where you can be attentive.

- ***Encourage and Praise:*** Help boost the confidence of coworkers by acknowledging them when they speak at meetings, even with just a nod. Actively look for the good things people are doing and give praise for specific behaviours and actions. Praise reinforces what is expected and boosts morale among employees.

- ***Smile and Call People by Name:*** Smiling is contagious! If you smile at people in the workplace, it establishes your approachability and helps lift the general attitude of the workplace environment. When you talk to people in the workplace, get in the habit of calling them by name. If you also talk to them about things that interest them or their hobbies or use their family member's names, you will build stronger relationships as people feel valued and cared about.

Best Behaviour #4: Demonstrate a Positive Attitude

There is nothing like a positive attitude to make a good impression and prove your abilities for advancement! Your positive attitude, or lack of one, will determine whether or not you advance successfully in your career.

Part of having a positive attitude is taking pride in the work you do and having a passion for what you do. Understand that everything you do has your signature on it. When people complete tasks based on their skills and knowledge but without taking pride in what they're doing, the work may be completed, but there's a good chance that it is of mediocre quality. Having passion for your work will help you through challenging and difficult times in the workplace and give you enthusiasm for getting it done because you believe it's worth doing and worth doing to the best of your ability.

How to Show Off a Positive Attitude in the Workplace

- *Be Aware of How You Carry Yourself:* It all starts with the first impression. To be perceived as positive you have to appear to be friendly, approachable, and looking at things generally in a positive way. Be aware of how you react to a negative situation and maintain your composure and be confident in your ability to deal with it or with the company's ability to survive the situation. If you are in a supervisory or executive position, others will be watching you, and if you demonstrate a positive attitude so will they.

- *Volunteer for What No One Else Wants:* Having a positive attitude is demonstrated when you are willing to take on assignments and projects that no one else wants to do. It shows you're willing to try to learn new things and improve the competitive advantage for the company.

- *Be an Action Taker:* There are many people who will create a plan and even draw it up on paper and know exactly how everything will play out but who never take action. Be an action taker and ensure that the entire plan has a person assigned to each task in the process. If you are the person assigned, make sure you deliver what is expected.

- *Learn to Effectively Multitask:* Not everyone can manage more than one task at a time, but if you hope to advance in your career successfully, the ability to multitask is going to help you considerably. Companies are looking to deliver more with less; the economy makes it impossible for most companies to hire someone to fill every role individually, and it becomes expected that employees can handle more than one project or task at a time. When accomplished, this actually becomes an asset to the company and can give them a competitive advantage.

- *Accept Personal Responsibility:* Having a positive attitude in the workplace requires that you accept personal responsibility for your work at all times. Don't look for others to blame or make excuses for anything you do that is less than satisfactory. When you own up to mistakes you make and learn from your mistakes, you are setting a good example for others and showing that you are responsible for your actions. When someone else in the organization does something well, give credit where credit is due. Never accept credit for the tasks someone else has done.

Best Behaviour #5: Act Like a Role Model

Whether you know it or not, people are always watching what you do. When you are demonstrating a positive attitude, making good decisions, and doing what is right, your peers will look at you as a positive role model (even if they themselves don't realize it's happening!). Being a role model is not always easy. Chances are you may get teased at times for always doing the right thing, but that doesn't mean people don't respect you and look up to you. When you have respect for yourself and believe in yourself, you are probably going to stand out from the crowd, and that's a good thing when you are building a career. Having a vision for improving your life and working toward that vision will result in you becoming a positive role model for others.

Standing out from the rest may make you feel as though you don't fit in. The truth is that you're not supposed to "fit in." Being unique is what gives you the opportunity for career advancement, and being a positive role model requires you do your best day after day and learn from your mistakes on the journey.

The Characteristics of a Positive Role Model

Wondering if you are a positive role model? If you have the following characteristics, chances are people look up to you as a role model. If not, make it a point to develop these character traits.

- ***Show How and Why You Make Decisions:*** Whenever you are presented with a challenge and need to make a decision, think out loud. This allows your coworkers or employees to experience your decision-making process. When you talk through your thinking process, they can see how you work through problems and weigh the pros and cons of each situation and finally how you come to the final decision. It's not only important what decision is made, but why the decision was made the way it was.

- ***Accept Responsibility for Mistakes:*** Good role models make mistakes— everyone does. It's part of being human. What sets a good role model apart from the rest of the population is that they're willing and able to accept responsibility when they make mistakes, learn from those mistakes, and let everyone see what they've learned and how they've corrected it.

- ***Be Someone Who Follows through Until the End:*** A good role model will demonstrate an ability to follow through to completion on everything they start. You need to be on time, finish everything you start without quitting when the going gets tough, and keep going despite challenges and difficulties.

- ***Be Confident and Proud:*** Setting a good example for others involves having confidence in yourself and being proud of what you've chosen to do with your life.

- ***Go Outside Your Comfort Zone:*** Success is found by reaching beyond your current comfort zone and through becoming a lifelong learner. The more you challenge yourself, the higher your success will be. Going outside your comfort zone also sets a good example for those whom you are hoping to impress and encourages improved performance.

- ***Be Respectful at All Times:*** Good role models and individuals seeking career advancement are driven, intelligent, and rarely take no for an answer, but they must also be respectful.

Best Behaviour #6: Always Do What You Say You Will Do

Being successful requires dependability. Your coworkers and management must know you will do what you say you will do without making excuses. If the circumstances should change at some point and you are somehow unable to do what you said you would do, apologize. Make other arrangements for the task to be completed.

Part of being reliable and dependable is also being on time. Don't be the person who shows up five or ten minutes late to work every morning or strolls in after a meeting starts. If being on time is a challenge for you, plan to be at every event thirty minutes before it starts. If you eventually learn to show up early, so be it! It's always better to be a little early than to always be late.

Plan to complete work tasks before the deadline. Note deadlines on your calendar so you won't forget them, and review your work in progress daily to make sure you're on track to finish on time. When you submit work make sure it is the best possible work you can do, every time. While you want to get in the habit of completing projects ahead of schedule, you don't want to sacrifice the quality of your work to finish the assignment early.

Best Behaviour #7: Treat Others the Way You Want to Be Treated

This is also known as the "Golden Rule": you should always treat everyone the way you would want to be treated. Even take it a step further and treat people how *they* want to be treated. It's not always about what you give people; it's about understanding what other people want and then learning to give those services. It requires listening to what people say (and even what they don't say).

Best Behaviour #8: Find Out How Things Are Going

Don't wait for people to give feedback. Ask for feedback. Include phone numbers on everything you send out, and invite people to call you with questions or comments. Call people directly and ask how everything is going or whether they are satisfied with the service or products you've provided. Engage with everyone you do business with and listen to what is being said and use it as feedback. Be aware that how you respond in these feedback giving moments reflects the value you place on customers or coworkers.

If you can't engage feedback from people, observe what they do or say. Regardless of how you get the feedback (actively or passively), use it to understand the needs of your coworkers and customers. Tailor your service offerings and products so that they meet those needs.

Best Behaviour #9: Be Approachable

If you scare everyone off, you're not going to advance in your career! You need to develop an approachable attitude so that building relationships is possible. Not only do you need to learn how to approach other people; you also need to have a welcoming personality so that others feel comfortable approaching you.

Being approachable is all about your attitude. If you're confident in yourself, are enthusiastic, and smile, people will find it easier to approach you. Make sure that you are easy to get in touch with too, and don't make people feel as though contacting you is a bother or frustration for you.

Best Behaviour #10: Be Fair

Being fair means you're willing and able to take action even if it means not always being "nice." Everyone should always be treated equitably, and you should approach each situation with consistency in how you make decisions. To be fair, you must evaluate all information available before making judgments or decisions and approach situations with an open-mindedness. Being fair is also a telltale sign of your integrity, and whether you think so or not, others are watching.

Best Behaviour #11: Playing Office Politics without Manipulation

The definition of playing politics in the office environment is to deal with people in a manipulative or devious way in order to advance in the job or benefit yourself in some other way. While you want to advance your career and improve yourself, you don't want to do it through manipulation or devious methods. You can use "office politics" to build relationships that help you accomplish more than you could on your own but without hurting others in the process. The fact is that all organizations have their own "politics" involved, and you can't just swear not to get involved if your goal is to advance in your career. Instead, you need to learn how to work within your company's political structure in a positive way. A manager I knew was frustrated that whenever he went to talk to the manager from the department he provided a service to he received a cold shoulder. There were a number of process issues that this manager had identified that could be dealt with if the two managers worked together, but to date that didn't seem possible. It turned out that this manager was young and obviously on the fast track for promotion and the other manager was jealous that his career was not advancing; accordingly, he wasn't going to help others. The manager decided that instead of approaching the second manager with the issues first that he would spend time trying to get to know him and build a personal relationship. He also identified some knowledge that the second manager was known to have and approached him and asked if he would teach and coach him in that area. The second manager felt that he was being respected and decided to teach the first manager on the topic. In short order their relationship had been developed to the point that the two managers could work together to solve the original issues.

A supervisor I also knew was confronted with a similar situation as the manager in the story above, except when confronted with resistance from the second supervisor he decided to go over his head and approach his manager to report that this supervisor was not being cooperative. The result of this situation was that the second supervisor got in trouble with his boss and when forced to deal with the issues at hand was totally uncooperative and offered only one solution, which required a significant number of changes be made all in the first supervisor's area. Going forward, the second supervisor was not interested in pursuing any further interaction with this supervisor and it became almost impossible for a positive relationship to be developed.

Understanding office politics and using them positively to advance your career involves knowing how success is measured in your workplace. Is it increasing the company profits? Is it providing outstanding customer service or receiving customer testimonials from satisfied customers? Figure out what is considered successful within the organization and then take steps to fulfill the tasks that are considered to lead to success.

Best Behaviour #12: Don't Gossip or Spread Rumours

Every workplace has a rumour mill or gossip. Unfortunately, when rumours are spread, an employee's reputation or character can be damaged, even when the rumours aren't true. Impacted employees' productivity will suffer as they will feel they work in a hostile environment. Do not spread rumours or gossip about coworkers or your employees under any circumstances, and take personal responsibility to control the spread of rumours in the workplace.

The best way to put an end to unproductive office gossip or rumour spreading is through good communication. Be an effective communicator with your team; teach others good communication skills so that trust develops; address rumours that start as quickly as you hear them; and help keep everyone's head in the game.

Best Behaviour #13: Learn to Control Negativity

You've probably heard the saying "The rich get richer," right? The idea of that saying is that what people have, they get more of. There are people who believe that what you think about is what you become or what you receive from the universe. Regardless of how it happens, it does seem to be true that positive thinking and positive emotions brings positive results, while people who are constantly dwelling on the negative emotions and thinking get nothing more than negativity in their lives.

When you learn to control negative thoughts and emotions, you can take control of the type of experiences you have. When you are focused on negative thoughts, take time to turn them around and reassess them. You'll probably discover much of the negativity involves irrational thoughts. When you're aware of the negative and irrational thoughts, you can challenge them and erase them or turn them into positive thoughts. Pay attention to all positive feelings and thoughts, because you then give yourself room to experience more of those feelings. When a negative situation occurs, people tend to dwell on it and how it negatively affects them. I have learned that the first thing that should be done is to try to put the situation into a much larger context. Doing so puts the significance of the situation into perspective. Doing this allows you to control your emotions and use logic and rationale to deal with it rather than negativity. If you supervise others and you see your employees fall into this negativity trap, you can help them by showing them the context as well as your attitude. This will help get everyone to work on a solution rather than just dwelling on the situation.

Best Behaviour #14: Be and Demonstrate Confidence

When you feel good about yourself and confident in yourself, you stand taller and move with purpose and people are attracted to your warmth and energy. When you're confident, it shows in your moods, your attitude, and your facial expressions. Confidence leads to stronger relationships and trust and being approachable. They all work together hand in hand.

Dwight D. Eisenhower said, "In order to be a leader, a man must have followers. And to have followers, a man must have their confidence."

Career advancement in the management track requires that you have confidence in yourself. If you lack confidence or doubt your abilities, you will struggle to influence others.

How to Increase Your Confidence in the Workplace

It's no secret that confidence is necessary to advancing in your career, particularly if you are looking to fulfill management roles in the organization. Here are some tips for increasing your level of confidence in the workplace.

- *Always Be Yourself:* Most people can tell if others are attempting to be someone they are not. Don't look to copy someone else's style or personality. Don't force your behaviours, but do try to improve your presentation skills so that you will feel comfortable and natural when speaking to others one on one or in groups.

- *Know What You're Talking About:* You can't know it all or be everything to everyone. Identify the things you need to know, learn everything you can about those particulars, and then focus on effectively communicating what you know. Rehearse and prepare so that you are clear about what you need to say, and your confidence will shine.

- *Practice and Training:* If you're not comfortable with public speaking but your position requires that you communicate with staff, customers, or coworkers, you'll need to improve your speaking skills. Not everyone is a natural-born public speaker, but you can receive training and practice what you learn to get the skills needed to speak confidently in front of groups. The more you practice speaking, the more confident you will become.

- *Focus on Others:* If you are self-conscious, you can't be confident. Take focus away from yourself by focusing on others. Give people your full attention, which will take the focus away from you and help increase your own confidence.

Tips for Getting Others to See Your Confidence

Richard Branson, founder of Virgin Group (record label, airline; a business billionaire), insists that confidence is not a character trait or something people have or don't have. Confidence is what other people see in you. He believes that projecting confidence as a leader is achieved through helping others believe in your confidence.

Here's how to increase other's perception of your confidence:

- Maintain strong eye contact.
- Speak slightly louder than your normal speaking voice.
- Know your subject material when you speak, and speak succinctly.
- Stand straight and hold your head up high.
- Smile.
- Dress professionally.

Best Behaviour #15: Appreciate Behaviours You Value

Being gracious and expressing your gratitude is required to advance in your career and for being a "good manager." When you thank someone for exhibiting behaviours you want to see repeated, it reinforces the behaviour. Some managers decide a "thank you" isn't necessary for employees who are doing an activity that is part of their job responsibilities, but people who are thanked are more likely to repeat the behaviours. Everyone likes to be appreciated and recognized for their efforts!

Thanking employees publically for behaviours you want to reinforce is also an opportunity for the desired behaviours to "spread." Thanking employees is an effective way to increase motivation and performance; however, it is critical not to overuse your recognition when it is not earned or the employees' involvement is not readily identifiable. Using recognition inappropriately will demean its value and render its effectiveness as useless.

Expressing gratitude when it's deserved also increases the likelihood that people will later forgive you when you make a mistake.

Summary: Regardless of your skill set and competencies, it is important to remember the behaviour basics; otherwise leaders may never get the chance to see what you have to offer. You may not be recommended for a different position or promotion if managers don't see you exhibiting behaviours that are valued by leadership. Don't let others negatively impact your career. Take hold of your behaviours and be the employee who stands out as an informal role model.

Chapter 8

Managing Your Career

When you're lucky enough to find yourself in a career that makes you happy, you can't just sit back and let things "happen." You can't wait for someone else to manage your career for you. You have to be prepared to take action, continue to sweat the small stuff, always be on the lookout for networking opportunities, and be prepared to reinvent yourself at any moment. No one can manage your career as effectively as you can. Here's how to take control of your career.

Never Stop Networking

Most people think of networking as a necessary task when job searching, but you need to continue networking and building relationships even after you've landed the position you want. People you network with may not even have anything to do with your current line of work, but the people you connect with may have connections that are valuable to you and your industry. Look for opportunities to expand your network and connections. Attend industry conferences, introduce yourself to executives from other businesses, and keep your eyes and ears open for opportunities or ways you can offer valuable information to people. Plan to attend events and functions sponsored by the company and attended by senior leadership. Volunteer to assist at events where senior leaders will be in attendance.

Networking isn't always about getting ahead. You can also use networking as an opportunity to help others start or propel their careers without expecting a favour in return. You'll feel good about helping others, and you never know when those connections will result in good things for your own career or the company down the road.

Do Your Research

Not only does continuous networking help you develop relationships and connections that may result in your ability to help others or be helped by others, but networking is a great way to obtain information or seek out mentors. While you certainly can't sit back and wait for someone else to manage your career (it will never happen!) you also don't want to make the mistake of trying to manage your career *alone.* Everyone is looking to advance his or her career, and those who are already established in their careers need guidance and encouragement from time to time. Everyone from the entry-level employee to the CEO needs a mentor and a network (either formal or informal) to provide support.

If you are seeking a new position within your current company or in a different company, find out what would make an individual successful in that position. What educational background is considered necessary in that position? What experiences, skills, and abilities lead to success in the position you desire? Be prepared to pursue the education and experiences, and be prepared to develop the skills and abilities necessary for success in the position you want.

If you're currently in a position that falls short of your dream career or if you are in a role that you dislike or is not suited to you, continue to do the best you can and absorb whatever information you can from the position. This is also a great opportunity for you to assess the specific attributes of the position that cause you to be uncomfortable or that you just don't like. Take note of these attributes and use the newfound information to assess any new position that you are seeking to see if that position has the same or similar attributes. Remember that there are always opportunities to learn something new, and the things you learn in this position may prove valuable to you when you do get the career opportunity you really want.

You can increase the value of your knowledge to an employer if you can demonstrate knowledge of technical advances the company is not currently using and how that technology would benefit the company if they were to implement it. Having external knowledge of potential improvements and advancements for the company can be an effective entry point for discussion with the business leaders and give you the upper hand against competitors for the available position. If your ideas for new technology will reduce costs for the company or improve their quality or the efficiency of their operations, you can bet the business leaders will be very interested to learn about it.

Get to Know Yourself

You can't communicate what you want unless you know what you want. And once you know what you want, don't be afraid to communicate it! Your dreams and personal values may change as you get older, so be prepared to do a self-assessment of your dreams, values, and skill set periodically. Understanding yourself and what you are good at as well as what you want to do with your life can help ease nervousness surrounding changing careers or moving from one industry to another.

Get to know yourself better than anyone else does: what kind of work excites you and why (what characteristics of the work really appeals to you); are you a doer, a planner, a problem solver, a people person, a strategist, a teacher, a coach, a supervisor, a manager, a loner, or a team member? Understanding yourself helps you choose the appropriate career path.

Does travel interest you; does dealing with the unknown attract you or cause you fear; is predictability important to you; is accomplishing something every day important, are you a fixer, a creator, a follower, a leader? Are your work hours important; is work environment important; do you want to deal with customers; do you avoid problems or do you like to solve them?

Once you know yourself and what you like and dislike, make sure you go out and ask about the position or career you are seeking and see how many of the characteristics you say are important to you exist in that position or career. When you find out, you then need to ask yourself some questions.

Does the career you had your eye on have characteristics that don't appeal to you? If so, are you okay pursuing that career and making a trade-off?

Don't pursue a position or career and expect that you can change it to suit your desires—the success factors are the success factors.

Once you get to know what positions or careers are best suited to you and your abilities and desires, then you need to be honest with yourself and determine if what you want even exists in your current workplace. If not, then you have a choice to make.

Prepare for Other Positions or Careers

If you know for sure that your current workplace is not going to offer you the career you want or you need to move into a different position within the company, you will want to use other available resources to define expectations of the position or career you're after.

Surround Yourself with People in the Career You Want: Network with people who are currently in the role you want to be in. For example, you could get friendly with managers of the department you intend to work in. You would be surprised at how much you can learn about the expectations of a position simply by talking to people who are already in it and really listening to what they say when they talk about their work. You can benefit from talking to people within the company you most want to work at as well as meeting people in similar positions with other companies.

Get Educated: If you don't already have a degree or educational background in a field related to your desired career, it might be a good idea to take some courses or pursue a degree program.

Know What You Can Offer the Company: Understanding the success competencies of the position or career you are interested in makes it possible for you to assess your own strengths and identify parallel experiences or skills that qualify you for advancement consideration. When you understand what you can offer the organization that others cannot, you can show leadership why they should move you into the position you are interested in.

Create Your Personal "Brand": Identify the competencies, skills, attributes, and behaviours that best represent what you have to offer. Look for opportunities in the business world to make your "brand" known or to establish a reputation for having this set of characteristics. Creating a brand for yourself involves identifying those key characteristics or strengths that you have and developing "your story" about your skill set, how you have used your skills to help the company or others, what successes you have had, and what key experiences you excelled in. Look for key leaders who are willing to help validate your key characteristics and accomplishments. Repeat, repeat, repeat what your brand stands for and make sure that you use your brand characteristics in your everyday activities both in the workplace and outside. Generally for a brand to be real, the characteristics that you say you possess have to be demonstrated all the time. Like any other brand, you are attempting to sell yourself based on what others perceive to be "your promise" based on how you have branded yourself. Your brand will follow you wherever you go and will play an important role in helping you get into the position you really want.

You now know the secrets to career advancement. You need to start by understanding yourself, your likes, your dislikes, what excites you, what you tend to avoid, what work-family balance you expect, and whether your company offers the types of positions that satisfy your needs. Unfortunately, some individuals take their formal education in a field that they later learn does not lead them to the career that they would like. These individuals have to make a choice between settling for what they can achieve with the education they have or going into their field and trying to make the best of it. Or do they pursue an education in the field that they want to move their career toward? Remember that sometimes you can't have it all. You have to be realistic about your career choices and your educational achievements. Don't expect to be given the career you choose if you haven't got anything to offer. The best way to get to where you want to is by being prepared, understanding what is needed to be successful in that role, and getting the education, experience, and competencies that you can sell for consideration.

People can have successful careers as an individual contributor or as a manager of people or as an executive. Every company needs talented people in all three roles. So now you have to decide which category best suits you and then explore the positions that you can pursue in that category. Don't forget to sense-check your perception of your targeted position. Talk to people already in those roles to find out what is really expected of them and how they spend their time. Once you have a clear target in mind, begin to look at your competencies and behaviours and get feedback from peers, direct reports, customers, or anywhere else to get a sense of how you are perceived. Monitor your behaviours; develop your competencies; go after the developmental experiences you need either in your company or through other means like volunteer groups or committees; and don't forget to tell people what you want. If you don't tell them what you want, they won't know and they will manage your career based on what is best for the company.

I hope I have met your needs and given you the insights you were looking for to help you manage your career. Remember that to be successful in any category you must continue to learn every day and become the person who, as everyone says "we can't afford to lose."

Good luck!

Selected References

Arredondo, Lani. *Communicating Effectively.* New York: McGraw-Hill Trade, 2000.

Booher, Dianna. *E-Writing: 21st Century Tools for Effective Communications.* Pocket Books, 2001.

Bossidy, Larry, Ram Charan, and Charles Burck. *Execution: The Discipline of Getting Things Done.* New York: Crown Business Publishing, 2002.

Campbell, Andrew, and Kathleen Sommers Luchs. *Core Competency Based Strategy.* Cengage Learning EMEA, 1997.

Collins, James C. *Good to Great.* New York: Harper Business, 2001.

Collins, James C., and Jerry I. Porras. *Built to Last.* New York: Harper Business, 1994.

Covey, Steven R. *The Seven Habits of Highly Effective People.* New York: Simon and Schuster, 1989.

Daniels, Aubrey C. *Performance Management.* Tucker, Georgia: Performance Management Publications, 1989.

Daniels, Aubrey C. *Bringing Out the Best in People.* McGraw-Hill, Inc., 2000.

Drucker, Peter F. *Managing for Results.* New York: HarperCollins, 1993.

Duncan, Peggy. *Put Time Management to Work: Get Organized, Streamline Processes, Use the Right Technology.* PSC Press, 2002.

Ellis, Albert, PhD. *How to Control Your Anxiety Before it Controls You.* Citadel Press 2000.

Goddard, J. "The Architecture of Core Competence." *Business Strategy Review* 1 (1997).

Hout, Thomas M., and John C. Carter. "Getting it Done: New Roles for Senior Executives."

Harvard Business Review, February 2000.

Huppe, Frank T. *Successful Delegation: How to Grow Your People, Build Your Team, Free up Your Time and Increase Profits and Productivity.* Hawthorne, N.J.: Career Press, 1994.

Hutchings, Patricia J. *Managing Workplace Chaos: Solutions for Handling Information, Paper, Time and Stress.* New York: AMACOM, 2002.

Kaplan, Robert S., and David P. Norton. *The Strategy-Focused Organization: How*

Balanced Scorecard Companies Thrive in the New Business Environment. Watertown,

MA: Harvard Business School Press, 2000.

Kerr, Steven, ed. *Ultimate Rewards.* A Harvard Business Review Book, Harvard Business School Press, Boston MA, 1997.

Lee, John H., and Bill Scott. *Facing the Fire: Experiencing and Expressing Anger Appropriately.* New York: Bantam Books, 1993.

Lombardo, Michael M., and Robert W. Eichinger. *For Your Improvement.* Lominger

Leadership Architect Suite, 2003.

Lombardo, Michael M., and Robert W. Eichinger. *The Leadership Machine.* Lominger

Leadership Architect Suite, 2003.

Mascarenhas, B., A. Baveja, and M. Jamil. "Dynamics of Core Competencies in Leading

Multinational Companies." *California Management Review* 40 (1998).

McKenna, Patrick J., and David H. Maister. *First Among Equals: A Guidebook for how Group Managers Can Manage the Unmanageable.* New York: The Free Press, 2002.

Prahalad, C. K., and G. Hammel. "The Core Competence of the Corporation." *Harvard*

Business Review, May-June 1990.

Schoemaker, Paul J. H. "How to Link Strategic Vision to Core Capabilities." *Sloan Management Review,* Fall 1992.

Ulrich, David, Jack Zenger, and Norm Smallwood. *Results-Based Leadership.* Boston Massachusetts: Harvard Business School Press, 1999.

Welch, Jack, and John A. Byrne. *Straight from the Gut.* New York: Warner Books, 2002.